Science Fair Success

# *Microscope Science Projects and Experiments*

## Magnifying the Hidden World

Kenneth G. Rainis

**Enslow Publishers, Inc.**
40 Industrial Road                    PO Box 38
Box 398                                      Aldershot
Berkeley Heights, NJ  07922   Hants GU12 6BP
USA                                                  UK

http://www.enslow.com

*For Jim and Marilyn Loughlin,*
*their love for each other—*
*over fifty years!*

*and*

*In memory of*
*Dee Anne Chapleau,*
*a shaper of young lives.*

## Acknowledgments

This book would not have become a reality without the loving support of my wife, Joan. Thanks to my partners at Neo/SCI: Kurt Gelke, Jean Coniber, and George Nassis, whose support is greatly appreciated. Special thanks to Ken Rando, who, as always, helped me with the electrons and contributed several beautiful illustrations. Special thanks to Michael Peres, Chair, Department of Biomedical Photography at Rochester Institute of Technology, who graciously helped me make some of the photomicrographs viewed in this book.

**Library of Congress Cataloging-in-Publication Data**

Rainis, Kenneth G.
    Microscope science projects and experiments : magnifying the hidden
    world / Kenneth G. Rainis.
        p. cm. — (Science fair success)
    Summary: Enumerates supplies, equipment, and procedures for microscopic
experiments in four areas, the common, the tiny, plants, and animals.
    Includes bibliographical references (p. ) and index.
        ISBN 0-7660-2090-8 (hardcover)
        1. Microscopy—Experiments—Juvenile literature. 2. Science
projects—Juvenile literature. [1. Microscopes. 2. Microscopy—
Experiments. 3. Experiments. 4. Science projects.]
    I. Title. II. Series.
    QH278.R35 2003
    507.8—dc21

                          2002152976

Printed in the United States of America

10 9 8 7 6 5 4 3 2 1

**To Our Readers:** We have done our best to make sure all Internet Addresses in this book were active and appropriate when we went to press. However, the author and the publisher have no control over and assume no liability for the material available on those Internet sites or on other Web sites they may link to. Any comments or suggestions can be sent by e-mail to comments@enslow.com or to the address on the back cover.

**Illustration Credits:** Jacob Katari, p. 13; Kenneth G. Rainis, pp. 29, 31, 44, 47, 55, 61, 64, 66, 68, 73, 77, 78, 82, 85, 90, 94, 99, 102, 105, 108, 110, 113, 115, 117, 122; Ken Rando, pp. 6, 15, 16, 18, 23, 26, 52; National Museum of Health & Medicine, Armed Forces Institute of Pathology, (MIS 66-1836-1) p. 7, (MIS 66-6248) p. 11, (MIS 60-4713-331) p. 36, (MIS 74-6716) p. 62, (MIS 66-6192) p. 92; Courtesy Neo/SCI Corporation, Rochester, NY, pp. 34, 38, 39, 41, 57, 58, 81, 97, 120.

**Cover Photo:** Kenneth G. Rainis

# Contents

# Witness to a Demonstration

It was a morning in April 1663, as members of the British Royal Society gathered at Gresham College, London, to witness a demonstration by the Curator of Experiments and member of the Royal Society—Robert Hooke. A tall, barrel-shaped instrument stood before them on a table near a south-facing window. Next to it was a device to provide additional light. The oil lamp wick was carefully trimmed to produce a strong, yellow light. The Royal Society members could see that the light was focused through a lens to concentrate it onto a thin piece of oak cork. The cork rested on a black object that was impaled on a pin resting on a "stage."

Hooke told the members that the microscope before them was of his design, made by the noted London instrument maker Christopher Cock. He then demonstrated how, through careful adjustment, a very "satisfactory" image could be observed.

Hooke spent the better part of the morning allowing members of the society to view this section of cork tissue by peering into the eyepiece. He explained that the lens system of his microscope magnified objects as much as fifty times larger than if they were viewed with the eye alone. He also pointed out that the microscope could be used as an investigative tool to understand the properties of cork: its lightness, compressibility, and ability to float.

Like those members of the Royal Society, you can look through the lenses of microscopes today to better understand the world of small things.

## How This Book Is Organized

This book contains activities that center on using a microscope or magnifying glass (also known as a single-lens

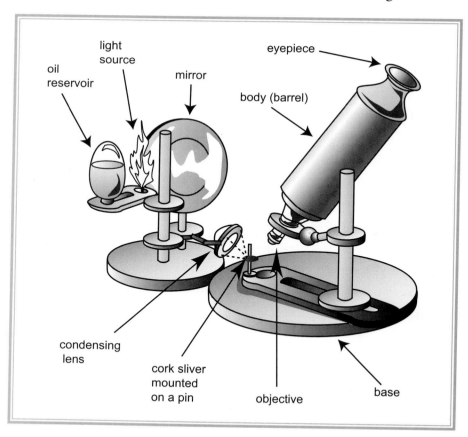

Hooke's microscope as it was presented in his book *Micrographia*.

## Robert Hooke (1635–1703)

Robert Hooke was perhaps the single greatest experimental scientist of the seventeenth century. He designed a compound microscope and illumination system, one of the best such microscopes of his time. He was the author and illustrator of the first picture book of science—*Micrographia* (small things), published in January 1665. The book contains the results of a series of sixty observations and experiments conducted between 1661 and 1664. Part of the world's fascination with *Micrographia* was that it opened up a new—small—world for everyday people to explore.

microscope) to view details about small things that our eye, alone, cannot. Just as in Hooke's *Micrographia*, you have the opportunity to do microscopic explorations. Some are historical, duplicating the methods and observations of great microscopists. Others will give you an opportunity to learn more about the world around you, most of it invisible without the microscope. They will help you answer the question posed in each exploration. There are also suggested science fair ideas. Appendix A gives you more information about additional ways of preparing specimens and samples, along with special lighting methods for microscopic observation.

## Recording, Analyzing, and Reporting Your Observations

The microscope will become an indispensable tool for collecting visual information for this book's science project investigations. To be useful, visual data must be recorded. Keep a notebook to write down your observations. Be sure to include the date, time, viewing magnification, and sample preparation method used. Also list the source of the specimen material that you observed. Just where did that jar of green water come from? Get in the practice of making drawings that illustrate what you are observing. Learn to draw just the key features that will help support your written observations.

Reporting your observations and conclusions in a clear manner is critical to your success as a scientist. Your science fair project report should contain the following parts and be in this order:

I. STATEMENT OF PROBLEM. What are you trying to find out?

II. BACKGROUND. Information that relates to the question. Include a bibliography with at least three references.

III. HYPOTHESIS. What is a possible answer to your question? What do you think might happen?

IV. EXPERIMENTAL DESIGN OR PROCEDURE. Describe how you will test your hypothesis. Include all the steps you will follow and include drawings or photographs to help in this explanation. Make sure that you design a controlled experiment and can identify the planned change—the variable or variables—in the experiment.

V. RESULTS. List all the information (data) collected during the experiment or microscopic observation. Use charts, graphs, photographs, or drawings to help organize data for easier understanding.

VI. CONCLUSIONS. How does what happened compare to what you thought would happen?

Check with your science teacher to see whether your science fair has a different format for reports. Either way, be very neat. The report should be typed or written clearly in blue or black ink.

## Project Display

Check with your science teacher for your fair's rules on project displays. Presenting and displaying your project at school will usually require you to use a display board.

## Tools You Will Need

Most of the tools you will need for your explorations can be found around the house. There are many inexpensive microscopes available (see Appendix A). You may also be able to use a microscope at school. Sources for other items are listed in Appendix B. The most essential tool, of course, is your curiosity!

## Being Safe

Ten rules to keep you safe:

1. Be serious about science. A careless attitude can be dangerous to you and to others.

2. Never look directly into a lens pointed at the sun. Doing so can cause serious injury to your eyes.

3. Read instructions carefully and completely before proceeding with any activity outlined in this book. When expanding on these activities, discuss your experimental procedure with a knowledgeable adult before proceeding. A flaw in your design could produce an accident.

**If in doubt, check with a science teacher or other knowledgeable adult.**

4. Keep your work area clean and organized. Never eat or drink while conducting experiments.

5. Microscopes are precision optical instruments. Keep your microscope clean. Use care when examining liquids. Immediately wipe up any spill.

6. Wear protective goggles when doing activities involving chemicals, heating objects or water, or when performing any other experiment that could lead to eye injury.

7. Do not touch chemicals with your bare hands unless instructed to do so. Do not taste chemicals or chemical solutions. Do not inhale vapors or fumes from any chemical or chemical solution.

8. Clean up any chemical spill immediately. If you spill anything on your skin or clothing, rinse it off immediately with plenty of water. Then report what happened to a responsible adult.

9. Keep flammable liquids away from heat sources.

10. Always wash your hands after conducting activities. Dispose of contaminated waste or articles properly.

# Chapter 1

# *How We See Small Things*

## Robert Bancks (1780–1850)

Robert Bancks was a London instrument maker and optician who produced simple and compound microscopes dating from 1796. Bancks' skill in grinding and polishing lenses allowed many scientists of the day to observe crisp and sharp images that were magnified up to 170 times.

In this chapter you will explore what a lens is, how it magnifies an image, how to calculate the magnifying ability of a lens, and how microscopes help you to see the invisible world.

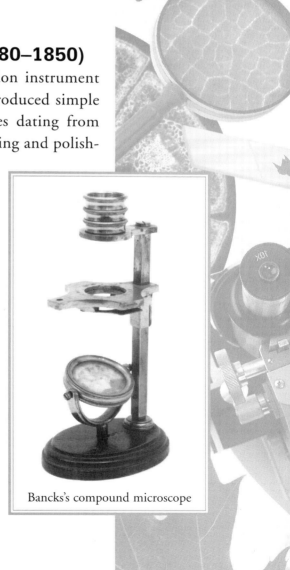

Bancks's compound microscope

# Exploration 1.1

## What Do Lenses Do to Light?

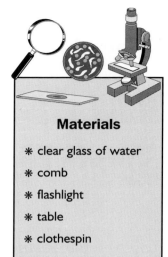

### Materials

- \* clear glass of water
- \* comb
- \* flashlight
- \* table
- \* clothespin

An image is what we see. Light strikes an object, bounces or is reflected off it, and enters our eye. The light is collected or focused by the eye's lens onto the retina at the back of the eye. There, the focused light stimulates special cells that send impulses to the brain. The brain assembles the object's image. Objects become visible to us when they are large enough to reflect light from a surface to our eye. So how can we see very small objects, like a bacteria cell? We use additional lenses to help our eye's own lens. The easiest way to learn about lenses and magnification is to do some simple activities.

Light generally travels in straight lines. A lens is a transparent object with at least one curved surface that bends light. Light entering the center of the lens goes straight through, but light entering at the curved edges gets bent toward the center (see Figure 1).

You can make a simple lens using a clear glass of water. You will observe the bending ability or "power" of this lens with a comb. In a darkened room, place a flashlight flat on a table so that the beam of light is visible on the table's surface. Now lay a clothespin flat on the table and use it to hold the comb in an upright position. Place the comb about 1 cm (1/2 in) in front of the flashlight lens so that the light shines through the teeth of the comb, creating many light beams. Now place a clear glass of water on the other side of the comb. Can you see light on the opposite side of the glass being bent inward toward the center, almost forming a point? Sketch your observations in your notebook.

Here, the glass of water is acting as a lens. Light striking the curved sides of the glass lens are bent inward. This bending, or refraction, of light is an important characteristic of lenses that allows them to focus a beam of light onto a single point.

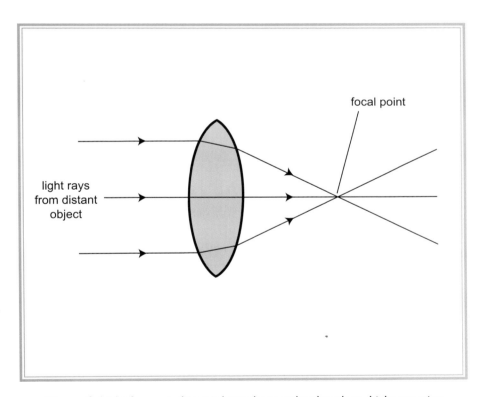

**Figure 1.** Light from an object is brought together by a lens. Light entering the center of the lens continues straight. Light entering the curved edges of the lens is bent toward the focal point.

# How a Lens Magnifies

**Materials**

* clear glass of water
* this book

Scientists define magnification as the apparent size of a magnified object divided by its true size. For example, if a lens produces an image of a viewed object to our eye that is four times its real size, its magnification capability or power is 4 divided by 1, or 4X.

Take a clear drinking glass and fill it almost to the top with water. Now take this book and place it behind your home-made lens. Look through the center area of the glass. Do the printed words on this page appear larger?

Your eye's lens is being helped by another lens—that of the curved surface of the drinking glass, which is spreading light rays that have bounced off the letters on this book's page. The letters appear larger.

## Understanding Magnifying Power

The magnifying power of a lens depends upon its focal length—the distance from the center of the lens to the point where the image is focused on a surface. Most people hold a book (or any other object) about 25 cm (10 in) away to see clearly when reading. This 25-cm distance is considered to be the focal length of our eye (see Figure 2a).

A lens with greater curvature has a shorter focal length and thus a greater magnifying ability. It refracts (bends) light rays more toward each other, and thus they meet at a shorter distance from the lens (see Figure 2b). The use of an additional lens helps our eye observe enlarged images.

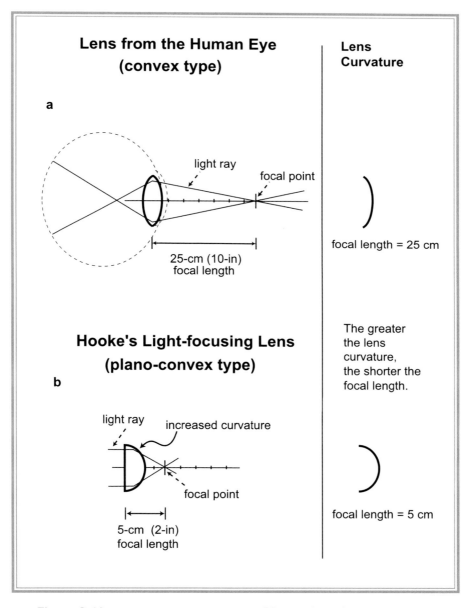

**Lens from the Human Eye (convex type)**

**Lens Curvature**

a

light ray

focal point

25-cm (10-in) focal length

focal length = 25 cm

**Hooke's Light-focusing Lens (plano-convex type)**

The greater the lens curvature, the shorter the focal length.

b

light ray    increased curvature

focal point

5-cm (2-in) focal length

focal length = 5 cm

**Figure 2.** UNDERSTANDING FOCAL LENGTH. Observe how the curvature of a lens affects its ability to focus light rays. a) The human eye has a convex type of lens with a focal length of approximately 25 cm (10 in). b) Hooke's light-focusing lens, a plano-convex type, has a shorter focal length—approximately 5 cm (2 in).

# Exploration 1.3

## Calculate a Lens's Magnifying Power

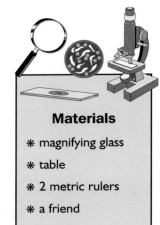

**Materials**

* magnifying glass
* table
* 2 metric rulers
* a friend

Hold a ruler upright on a table in one hand and a magnifying glass in the other hand, next to the ruler (see Figure 3). Peer through the magnifying glass and gradually lower it until a sharp focus is achieved. Have a friend observe the distance between the middle of the lens and the table's surface. This distance is the magnifying glass's focal length.

Calculate the magnification ability or "power" of the lens by dividing the focal length of the human eye (25 cm, or 10 in) by the focal length of the magnifying lens. For example, suppose a magnifying glass has a focal length of 5 cm. Its magnification would be calculated as:

$$\text{Magnification} = \frac{25 \text{ cm} \text{ (focal length of human eye)}}{5 \text{ cm} \text{ (focal length of magnifying glass)}} = 5\text{X}$$

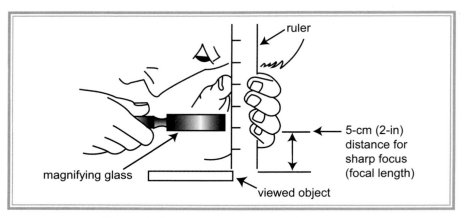

**Figure 3.** Calculating a lens's magnifying power.

# Exploration 1.4

# Observing Real and Virtual Images

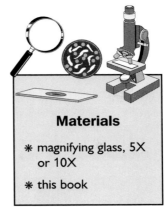

**Materials**

* magnifying glass, 5X or 10X
* this book

Pick up a magnifying glass and examine it with your clean fingers. Notice that both surfaces of the lens curve outward. The outward curvature of a lens makes it a convex lens (rounded like an oval); see Figure 4. You will use this double-convex lens to produce two kinds of images. It is called double convex because both sides of the lens are curved outward. Each side of the lens has a focal point.

Place this book flat on a desk. Stand up and hold the magnifying glass close to this page and about arm's length from your eye. Slowly lift the magnifying glass away from the page. The upright, enlarged image you see is called a virtual image. It is formed by light rays that spread out as they pass through the lens. Because the page is between the lens and its focal point on that side, the image appears to be on the same side of the lens as this printed page. A virtual image is always right side up (see Figure 4a).

Now move the magnifying glass farther away from this page, toward your eye, until the printed words appear upside down. The focal point for the page side of the lens is now between the page and the lens. This real image is formed when light rays from an object pass through the lens and both of its focal points are focused on the eye side of the lens. A real image is always upside down and reversed (see Figure 4b).

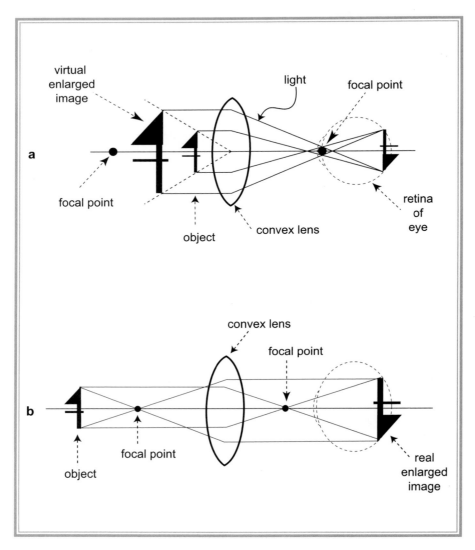

**Figure 4.** UNDERSTANDING VIRTUAL AND REAL IMAGES. a) Creating a virtual image. b) Creating a real image.

Exploration 1.5

# Constructing a Water Lens Microscope

## Materials

* paper punch
* index card, cut to 1 in x 3 in
* clear tape
* cup of water
* eyedropper
* this book

Use a paper punch to punch a center hole in a section of a 1-in-x-3-in piece of an index card. Next, carefully cover the hole with a piece of clear tape. Turn the card over.

Using an eyedropper, place a drop of water onto the clear tape in the hole. Keep adding small drops of water until the enlarging water drop fills the hole.

In your notebook, draw the shape of the water lens you just made. Compare this shape to the "condensing lens" that Robert Hooke used in his illumination system (page 6 and Figure 2b). What you have made is a plano-convex lens—*plano* means "flat" and *convex* means "curved like the outside of a sphere." One side of the water lens is flat (against the tape) and one side is curved.

Now observe how your lens magnifies. Carefully pick up the card and hold it over the type in this book. You should see a virtual image that is right side up and magnified. Can you create a real image with your water lens?

You should also notice a "blurring" or distortion around the edges of the image. This blurring problem plagued early microscopists, too. Over time lens makers learned to make better-quality glass without contaminants and imperfections that degraded image quality. They also found that compound lenses (two or more lenses fused together) helped reduce blurring. The lenses in a compound microscope are actually compound lenses.

## Science Fair Ideas

- Make liquid lenses out of other transparent materials. See if these materials bend light differently than water, causing the lens to have a different magnification ability. Try a mineral oil lens or an olive oil lens. Do these lens types have the same optical properties (focal length and magnification) as the water lens? Also try various thick, clear shampoos that contain glycerin.
- Construct a giant water lens by using a rectangular piece of acrylic as a transparent surface on which to build up a large water drop. Can you use this lens to observe details of large objects such as a flower or rock?

### Resolution Equals Information

Resolution is the amount of detail seen in an object. This is determined by how much an object's image is enlarged by a lens. Resolution is greatest at higher magnifications. At a certain fixed distance (about 25 cm, or 10 in), the lens of the human eye can resolve two small objects as separate points just as long as the two objects are farther apart than 0.2 mm.

Just like the eye, microscopes that use visible light have a limit to what they can resolve. A compound light microscope has a magnification ability of about 1,000X, and a limit of resolution, or the size of an object you can observe, of about 0.5 micrometer ($\mu$m). To see detail smaller than 0.5$\mu$m, you would need to use a beam smaller than visible light waves— such as a beam of electrons in an electron microscope.

*Note:* A micrometer is 0.000001 meter or 1/25,000 inch.

Exploration 1.6

# Test Your Eye's Resolving Power

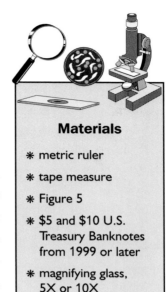

The eye examination chart that an optometrist uses is a test of the resolving power of the human eye at a distance of twenty feet. These activities will test your eye's resolving power at 25 and 122 cm (10 and 48 in).

## Resolution Activity 1

Hold this book at a normal viewing distance—approximately 15 cm (10 in). Now look at Figure 5. Can you read the entire six-line poem by Jonathan Swift? Use a metric ruler to measure the height of the type in the first line of the poem. The 9-point (pt) courier bold style type should measure 2 mm. A person with normal vision should be able to make out the individual 2-mm-high capital letters at a distance of 122 cm (48 in).

Prop this book on a shelf so that Figure 5 is clearly displayed at eye level. Use a tape measure to measure a distance of 122 cm (48 in) from the book page. At this distance, determine the line of capital letters of the poem that is no longer resolvable (that you can make out) with your eye. Line 2 of the poem has 8-pt letters, line 3 has 7-pt, and so on down to the last line of the poem, which has 4-pt capital letters that are less than 1 mm high. What capital letter height can your eye resolve at a distance of 122 cm (48 in)?

So Naturalists Observe,

A Flea Has Smaller

Fleas That On Him Prey;

And These Have Smaller Still

To Bite 'Em; And So Proceed

Ad, Infinitum.

**Figure 5.** Use this Jonathan Swift poem to test your eye's resolving ability.

Normal vision allows you to read the capital letters in the top line. If you can read any of the capital letters in the lower lines, you have better than normal visual sharpness. That means you can resolve a shorter distance than 2 mm.

## Resolution Activity 2

In 1999, $5 and $10 U.S. banknotes with new anticounterfeiting measures were introduced. Hold a banknote at eye level, approximately 25 cm (10 in) away from you. Look closely at the right and left areas under the oval portrait of Lincoln ($5 note) and directly on top of the word *Hamilton* (below his portrait in the $10 note). Can your eye resolve the microprinting that reads "The United States of America"?

Now look at these same areas using a 5X or 10X magnifying glass. Can you now resolve the letters and the words? Use your magnifying lens to scan the rest of the banknote for other areas where microprinting is used. You can also find microprinting on the signature line of most personal checks.

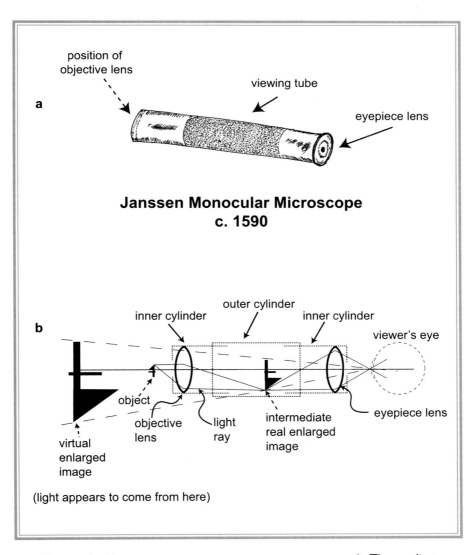

a

position of
objective lens

viewing tube

eyepiece lens

**Janssen Monocular Microscope
c. 1590**

b

outer cylinder

inner cylinder

inner cylinder

viewer's eye

object

objective
lens

light
ray

intermediate
real enlarged
image

eyepiece lens

virtual
enlarged
image

(light appears to come from here)

**Figure 6.** HOW A COMPOUND MICROSCOPE MAGNIFIES. a) The earliest compound microscopes consisted of an outer viewing tube into which two inner cylinders—each containing a lens—were inserted. b) A REPRESENTATION OF HOW THE JANSSEN MICROSCOPE MAGNIFIES AN IMAGE. Here the lens closest to the object to be viewed (the objective lens) creates a magnified real image inside the viewing tube. This image, in turn, becomes the object for the second lens (the eyepiece) and the image created by it is the enlarged virtual image that is seen.

# What Is a Compound Microscope?

A compound microscope uses two or more lenses to magnify an object's image. These lens groups are usually placed in opposite ends of a "viewing tube."

The development of the earliest compound microscope is credited to Zacharias Janssen, an eyeglass maker who lived in Holland in the 1590s. This microscope consisted of two convex lenses placed at opposite ends of a sliding tube. One lens (the objective) is held closer to the object or specimen to be viewed; the other lens (the eyepiece), closer to the observer's eye.

The compound microscope achieves a two-stage magnification. The objective lens projects a magnified image into the body tube, and the eyepiece lens further magnifies it. The objective lens has a longer focal length than the eyepiece lens.

The magnifying power of a microscope is determined by multiplying the magnification of the eyepiece by that of the objective lens. For example, if you used a 5X eyepiece with a 10X objective lens you would see objects magnified 50 times (5 x 10 = 50).

Exploration 1.7

# A Closer Look at Newsprint

**Materials**

* compound microscope, with light source
* newsprint
* ruler
* scissors
* microscope slide
* paper, 100% rag content

Most compound microscopes available in schools have a 10X eyepiece and three objective lenses: a 4X low-power scanning lens, as well as 10X medium and 43X high-power dry magnification (called high dry objective) lenses.

Use care when moving a compound microscope. Pick up and transport the instrument using two hands—one hand under the microscope's base and the other on the arm. Position the microscope on a flat surface, away from table edges.

Use Figure 7 as a guide when using a compound microscope to examine newsprint.

1. Make sure that the low-power (4X) objective is in place over the hole in the stage.

2. Use the coarse-focus knob to raise the 4X objective, from its lowest point, to about 2.5 cm (1 in) from the stage by turning the knob counterclockwise. This allows room for placing the sample on the stage for viewing.

3. Use scissors to cut a 25-mm (1-in) square piece of newsprint having lines of type. Place the newsprint on a clean microscope slide. Place the slide on the stage and orient it so that it is readable when looking at it

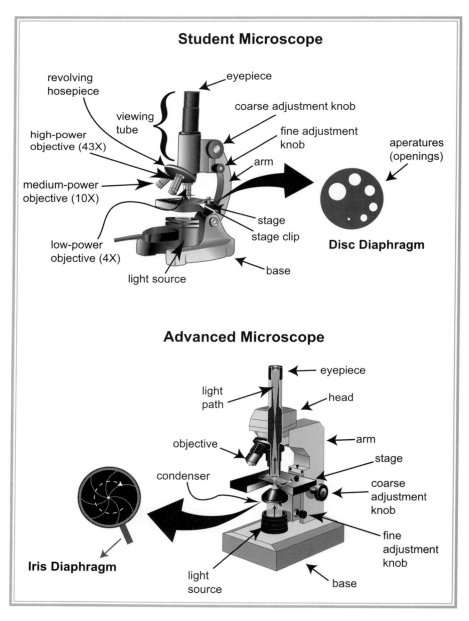

**Figure 7.** THE COMPOUND MICROSCOPE. a) Student microscope with a disc diaphragm. b) Advanced microscope with an iris diaphragm. Compare the light path trace in the diagram to that in Figure 6. *Note:* These microscopes may have a mirror instead of a powered light source.

without the eyepiece. Adjust the position of the newsprint so that it is over the hole in the stage. Use stage clips to secure the microscope slide on the stage.

4. Adjust the mirror or other light source to send light through the newsprint sample. Look through the eyepiece; you should be able to observe an even, bright circle of light.

   **Safety: Never use a microscope mirror to reflect direct sunlight—it could damage your eyes.**

5. Watching from the side, carefully lower the objective, moving it downward toward the newsprint, as close as possible, by turning the coarse adjustment knob clockwise.

6. Look through the eyepiece and use the coarse adjustment knob to *focus upward*, away from the microscope stage and the newsprint. Try to bring the sample image into rough focus. If you go too far, begin again at Step 5.

7. Use the fine adjustment knob to bring the image of the newsprint into sharp focus. Look in the eyepiece and observe how the lines of type look to your eye. Is the image upside down and reversed? Carefully move the newsprint sample around on the stage to obtain the best overall field of view. If you move the newsprint to the right, does the image move in the same direction?

8. Controlling the amount of light that passes through the sample—what microscopists call contrast—is important for proper viewing. Too much light (or flare) washes out the image, making it hard to see detail. A device called the iris diaphragm—similar to the iris of your own eye—controls this cone of light. Adjust the

iris diaphragm for best lighting. You will need more light (a wider diaphragm opening) at higher magnifications. Best contrast occurs as the field of view just begins to darken as you observe it through the eyepiece. If you close the iris too much, the viewing area will appear dark and muddy—the light is being sent through too small an opening.

*Note:* Some compound microscopes have a disc diaphragm instead of an iris diaphragm—a series of large to small circular openings on a wheel that can be moved to restrict the light beam (see Figure 7).

9. To switch to a higher magnification, carefully turn the revolving nosepiece and bring the next higher power objective (10X) into position over your sample. You will feel a click or bump as the new objective locks into place. You should only have to use your fine adjustment knob, focusing upward, to achieve a sharp focus. Remember: Never focus downward. It could drive the objective into your slide and damage the slide and the objective!

10. View the newsprint at the highest magnification you can. Be sure to adjust the iris or disc diaphragm for best contrast. Can you observe individual wood fibers? They are shaped like tiny toothpicks (see Figure 8).

11. Although most paper is produced from the wood of trees, finer papers have a lot of cotton fibers in them. The amount of cotton fibers in paper is sometimes called the rag content, since the fibers once came from old cotton rags that were recycled to make paper.

   Carefully tear a piece of fine 100 percent rag content paper to expose individual cotton fibers. Place the paper in the center of a clean microscope slide. Place another clean microscope slide on top of the sample creating a sandwich preparation. Examine the paper's ragged edge under medium (100X) magnification. Fine rag papers are made of cotton fibers, while newsprint is made of wood pulp. Some papers are made using both fiber types. Use Figure 8 to help you tell the difference.

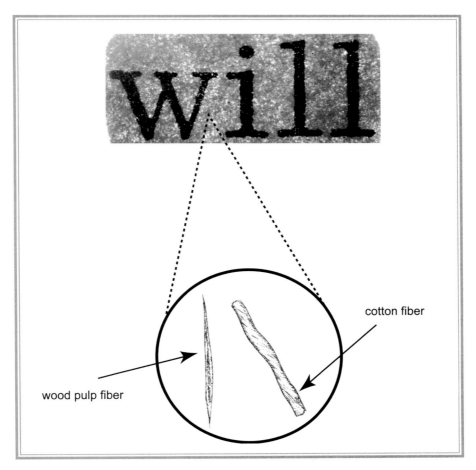

**Figure 8.** What is newsprint? Newsprint and other printing papers are made from either wood pulp or cotton fiber, or a combination of both.

12. When you have finished microscopic viewing, remove your sample and position the lowest-power objective over the hole in the stage. Turn off the light. Cover the microscope and put it in a safe place.

## Science Fair Ideas

- Compare printed type, such as the type in this book, laser printing, and inkjet printing to newsprint. Make drawings of your observations in your notebook.

- Examine several 2.5-cm (1-in) square pieces of newsprint from the comics page. Can you observe a dot pattern at various magnifications? Compare your observations of printed dot patterns using a compound microscope with observations using the single-lens water microscope in Exploration 1.5.

### Microscope Care

- If your microscope lenses get dirty, you may observe small flecks and spots in the field of view that remain stationary when you move the sample. To clean lens surfaces, always use lens tissue purchased at camera stores.

- Store your microscope covered in a safe, dry place, where it will not be knocked over. If your microscope has batteries, remove them before long periods of storage.

# Exploration 1.8

# A Closer Look at the Dot of an *i*

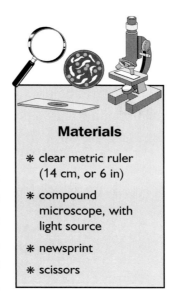

## Materials

* clear metric ruler (14 cm, or 6 in)
* compound microscope, with light source
* newsprint
* scissors

Place a clear plastic metric ruler on the microscope stage, and adjust the focus so that the scale is clearly in view at low (40X) magnification. Line up the 1-cm mark with the very left edge of your field of view. In your notebook, record the distance from the left edge to the right edge; see Figure 9. The width of the viewing area, or field diameter, at 40X magnification (10X eyepiece with a 4X objective lens) is approximately 4 mm (4,000 μm) wide.

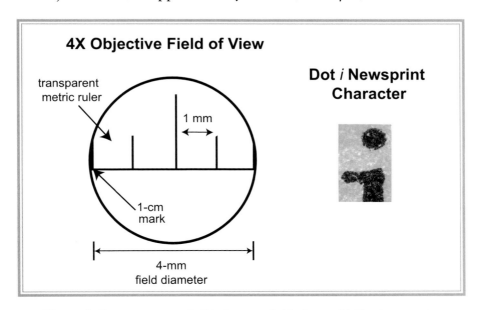

**4X Objective Field of View**

transparent metric ruler

1 mm

1-cm mark

4-mm field diameter

**Dot *i* Newsprint Character**

**Figure 9.** FIELD DIAMETER. a) 4X objective field of view. b) Dot *i* newsprint character.

The field diameter multiplied by the total magnification of the microscope will give you a mathematical constant. This constant can be used to calculate the field diameter for other combinations of eyepiece and objective magnifications. In this instance the constant would be calculated as:

| 4 mm (field diameter) | x | 10 (eyepiece magnification) | x | 4 (objective magnification) | = | 160 (constant) |

| Table 1. Field Diameters for Varying Magnification ||||
| Eyepiece Magnification (A) | Objective Magnification (B) | Calculated Constant (C) | Calculated Field Diameter $\dfrac{C}{A \times B}$ |
| --- | --- | --- | --- |
| 10X | 4X | 160 | 4 mm (measured) |
| 10X | 10X | 160 | 1.6 mm |
| 10X | 43X | 160 | 0.37 mm |

Once you know the field diameter, you can easily estimate a viewed object's size. For example, if an object takes up three-fourths of a 1.6-mm field diameter, it would measure approximately 1.2 mm.

Let's put your measuring skills to the test. Examine a piece of newsprint containing the letter *i*. Can you determine the size of the *i*'s dot?

## Science Fair Idea

Use your knowledge of microscopic field size to compare the sizes of the same character in different fonts. A font is a set of type characters of the same design. Use a computer word processing program to create text blocks using different fonts.

Exploration 1.9

# Demonstrating Hooke's Cells: Making a Wet Mount

**Materials**

* cork
* container
* water
* small weight
* vegetable peeler
* eyedropper
* microscope slide
* toothpick
* plastic coverslip
* compound microscope, with light source

Let's use Hooke's microscopic demonstration to understand the unusual properties of cork: its lightness, compressibility, and ability to float.

Cork is the tough outer bark of the European cork oak tree *Quercus suber*. It grows in Portugal, Algeria, Spain, Morocco, France, Italy, and Tunisia. The cork oak is the only tree whose bark can regenerate itself after the cork is harvested—leaving the tree unharmed.

Obtain a piece of cork. It will probably be dry. You will need to be able to pass light through this plant tissue, so it will have to be cut, or sectioned. To prepare a thin section for viewing, like Hooke did in 1663, place the cork piece in a cup of water. Observe what happens! You will need to weigh down the cork piece so that water can seep in over time and moisten its tissues. Let the cork sit in water for a couple of days.

Remove the dampened cork from the water. Holding the cork piece in one hand, use a vegetable peeler to shave thin pieces from it. Do not be surprised if you can only obtain small, crumbly pieces. Try to slice as thin a section as possible. (You can practice on a potato.) Watch as shaved pieces accumulate along the blade of the vegetable peeler. When you have a number of thin sections, carefully lay down the peeler.

## Making a Wet Mount

Using an eyedropper, place a drop of water in the center of a clean microscope slide. Dip an end of a toothpick into water to moisten it. Use this wetted end to pick up a small piece of shaved cork from the blade of the peeler. Transfer the cork section to the drop of water on the microscope slide. Carefully add a coverslip to make a wet-mount preparation of the cork section. Try to avoid air bubbles. To do this, slowly lower the coverslip at an angle on the drop so that any air bubbles will slide off the coverslip and escape. If the cork section is too thick, you may need to add a small drop of water under the coverslip.

Place the prepared section of cork tissue on the stage of a compound microscope. Bring the section into focus at low scanning power (40X magnification). Adjust the lighting. Your section will probably be too thick for light to pass through its center, so look for a ragged edge off to the side. Increase the

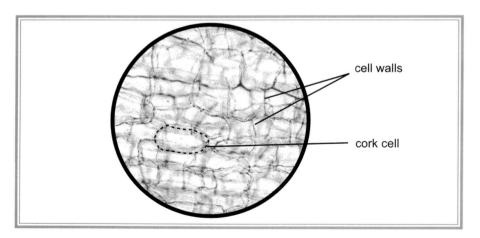

**Figure 10.** Cork cells at 320X.

magnification to medium power (100X) by bringing the 10X objective into the optical path. Again, adjust the lighting. Carefully focus on the ragged edge of the specimen. Compare what you observe to the image of a professionally made cork section in Figure 10. Can you estimate the size of your cork cells? (See Exploration 1.8 to estimate an object's size.)

Based on your observations, do you come to the same conclusions about cork as Hooke did? He deduced that the meshwork of empty spaces makes cork lightweight, compressible, and buoyant. Hooke named these air spaces "cells" because they reminded him of the small cells, or rooms, in monasteries. Hooke viewed cork tissue cells at a magnification of about 50X. This is what he wrote of his observations of cork:

> I could exceedingly plainly perceive it to be all perforated and porous, much like a Honey-comb, but that the pores of it were not regular. . . . these pores, or cells, . . . were indeed the first microscopical pores I ever saw, and perhaps, that were ever seen, for I had not met with any Writer or Person, that had made any mention of them before this.

Record your observations in your notebook. You may choose to write a report about your observations, just as Hooke did.

---

## Identifying Nature's Perfect Spheres—Air Bubbles

Many young microscopists have peered through the lens of a microscope and marveled at the round structures with thick, black walls—usually asking the teacher, "What organism is that?"

If that is what you see—you are probably looking at an air bubble!

---

Chapter 2

# From Cells to Crime Scenes

## Robert Brown (1773–1858)

A Scottish physician and botanist, Robert Brown observed and named the cell nucleus. He noted that it appeared in a wide range of living tissues. Through careful observations using a magnifying glass (single-lens microscope), he described the presence of "active molecules" and other microscopic phenomena.

In this chapter the microscope will allow you to explore many common and uncommon goings-on including the inner workings of cells, how light behaves, "active molecules" in milk, and how the microscope can help solve mysteries.

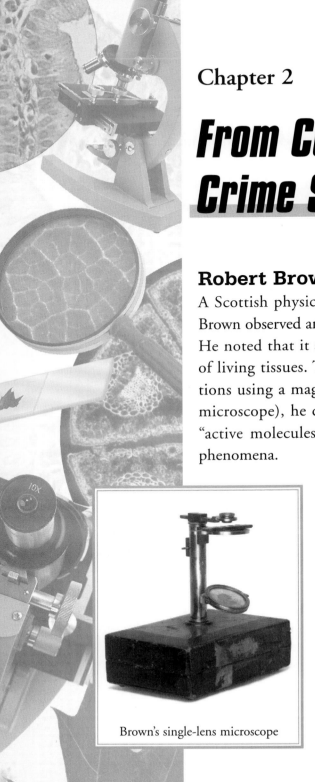

Brown's single-lens microscope

## Exploration 2.1

# How Big Is an Onion Cell?

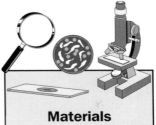

Safety: Use care when working with biological stains. Avoid skin and eye contact. Wear eye and hand protection.

In 1831, Robert Brown wrote about his observations of the nucleus in plants, pointing out that it occurred in every cell and tissue. Let's use the microscope to investigate a plant cell's nucleus and other plant cell structures.

Although the fleshy part of the onion grows underground, it is

**Materials**

* an adult
* small knife
* red onion pieces
* 2 eyedroppers
* microscope slide
* tweezers
* coverslip
* iodine stain
* disposable plastic gloves
* safety goggles
* compound microscope, with light source

actually made of specialized leaves. These leaves are thick because they are a food storage organ for the plant. The very thin layer of covering cells on the surfaces of these fleshy leaves are the epidermal layers, sometimes called the skin. **Ask an adult** to cut an onion into wedge-shaped pieces. Examine a piece of the cut onion and break it apart to expose a single leaf.

Place a drop of water in the center of a microscope slide. Use tweezers to remove the thin "skin" tissue layer from the thicker, fleshy part of the leaf and place it on the microscope slide. Add another drop of water (or iodine stain if available) over the onion epidermis and finish making a wet mount by adding a coverslip. The iodine will color internal cell structures, giving them extra contrast so that they are more visible.

Begin by examining the preparation at low-power (40X) magnification. You may need to reduce the lighting by using the disc or iris diaphragm.

Switch to 100X magnification. Using Figure 11 as a guide, can you observe cell nuclei and other cell structures in onion leaf cells? Estimate the size (length and width) of these onion cells at various magnification levels. Use Exploration 1.8 as a guide to microscopic measuring. Record your observations and measurements in your notebook.

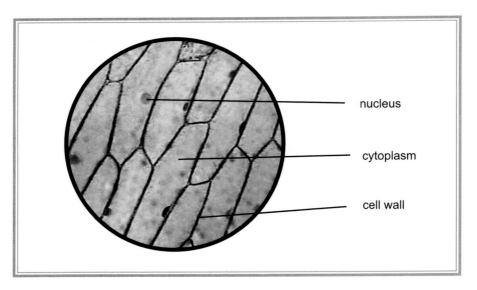

**Figure 11.** Onion cells at 430X.

## Science Fair Ideas

• Plant cells are filled with cytoplasm and have thick outer cell walls that help provide support. You can study the effect of a salt on the cytoplasm of these cells. Add 2 teaspoons of salt to a glass of water to create a concentrated salt solution. Make a wet mount of red onion epidermis. Use the "Moving Solutions" technique (see Appendix A) to introduce a salt solution to the onion cells. Observe the preparation at 100X. What happens to the cytoplasm inside the cells? Can you observe the cell wall more easily? What happens if you flush the salt water out using bottled water? Compare your observations with Figure 12.

• Obtain a white onion and prepare a wet mount of its epidermis. Compare the size of red onion cells to white onion cells. Which plant has larger cells?

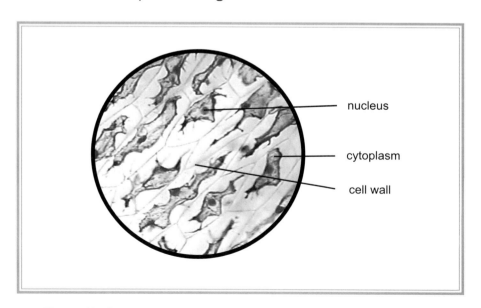

**Figure 12.** Onion cells in a salt solution, at 430X. What would you expect to happen to your epidermal (skin) cells if you stayed in the ocean surf for a long time?

## Exploration 2.2

# What Goes On Inside a Cell?

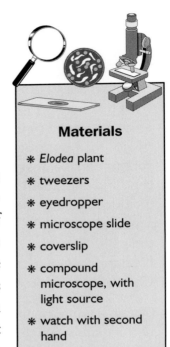

**Materials**

* *Elodea* plant
* tweezers
* eyedropper
* microscope slide
* coverslip
* compound microscope, with light source
* watch with second hand

Another discovery Robert Brown made with his single-lens microscope was the circulation of cytoplasm, or cell fluid. This process is called cytoplasmic streaming. He also discovered cell structures (organelles) such as chloroplasts. In this exploration you will find out just how fast organelles can move within a cell.

Obtain the aquarium plant *Elodea* at a pet or aquarium store. Use tweezers to remove a leaf from the growing tip of the plant. Make a wet mount by placing the leaf in a drop of water on a clean microscope slide. Add a coverslip and examine first at low (40X) magnification, then at higher magnifications. Be sure to adjust the iris or disc diaphragm to allow enough light to pass through the leaf. Carefully focus on a single *Elodea* cell. Compare your field of view with Figure 13. Measure these cells (use Exploration 1.8 as a guide). Are *Elodea* cells larger than onion cells?

Can you observe small, green, oval-shaped chloroplasts inside an *Elodea* cell? Do they travel around the cell in one direction or in a random fashion?

Use the second hand of a watch to time the movement of these organelles. How long does it take a chloroplast to make

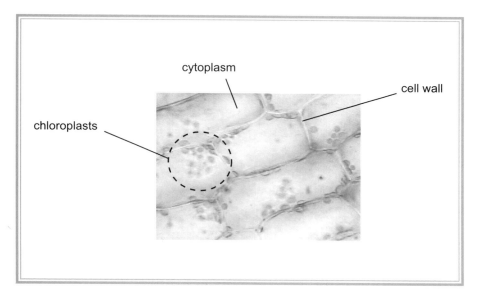

**Figure 13.** *Elodea* cells at 960X.

a trip around the interior of the plant cell? To obtain a rate (distance divided by time) of cytoplasmic streaming, divide the length of the cell (in micrometers) by the time it took a chloroplast to travel that distance (in seconds).

## Science Fair Idea

Duplicate Robert Brown's demonstration of cytoplasmic streaming in plant cells. You will need to obtain stamen hairs from the young flower of the wandering Jew (or spiderwort) plant, *Tradescantia virginiana*. Wandering Jews are common in florist shops or garden stores. Select a plant with small white flowers. Spiderwort flowers have stamen hairs. (These long hairs help ensure that pollinating bees deposit more pollen on the flower's stamen.) Stamen hair cells are one of the largest cells known. These hairs are actually strings of large, ball-shaped cells that contain blobs of fluid that travel along streams of flowing cytoplasm.

Use tweezers to extract a stamen hair from a flower. Make a wet mount and examine under high (430X) magnification. To see streaming more clearly, use interference lighting created by slipping a 1-in-x-3-in piece of index card over half the microscope illuminator. Again, be sure that you adjust the iris or disc diaphragm to allow enough light to pass through your preparation. Make small adjustments by moving the card in and out of the light path—pay careful attention to the light-dark interface produced by the edge of the card. See if your observations agree with Brown's:

> These cells are beautiful to observe: strands of cytoplasm are woven across cells, and tiny particles can be seen moving along in ordered rows.

## Exploration 2.3

# Just What Is Dust, Anyway?

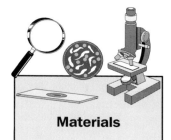

### Materials

* clear tape
* dust balls
* microscope slide
* tweezers
* eyedropper
* corn syrup
* coverslip
* pencil with eraser
* compound microscope, with light source

Dust is an accumulation of coarse and fine mineral grains, hair, microbe and plant spores, dead skin cells, and micro animals. Most of it falls as a film or in clumps on undisturbed surfaces, or is concentrated in vacuum cleaners.

Use clear sticky tape (2.5-cm, or 1-in, lengths) to pick up small dust balls and make a sticky mount by affixing the tape to a clean microscope slide.

Another examination technique involves making permanent mounts of collected dust balls. Use tweezers to pick up dust balls. Place a small piece of a dust ball in the center of a clean microscope slide. Use an eyedropper to place 2 to 4 drops of corn syrup on top of the dust mass. Add a coverslip. Use the eraser-end of a pencil to help spread the corn syrup by pressing on the top of the coverslip.

Examine dust ball preparations under scanning (40X), then medium (100X) magnification. Reduce the lighting to obtain maximum contrast (see Exploration 1.7, Step 8). Use Figure 14 as a guide to help you identify and classify dust ball components.

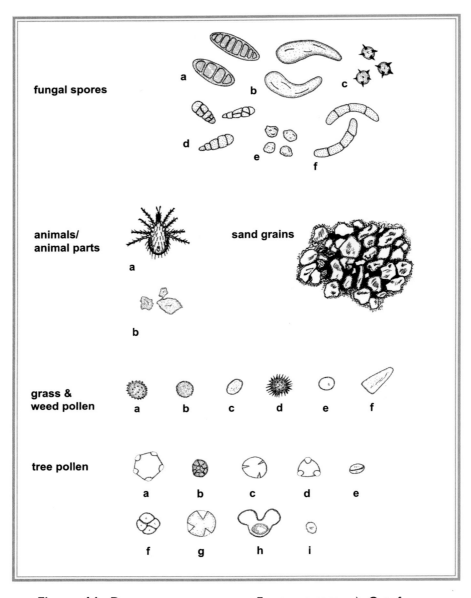

**Figure 14.** DUST BALL COMPONENTS. FUNGAL SPORES: a) Oat fungus, b) Mushroom spores, c) Rust fungus, d) Hay fever fungus, e) Black bread mold, f) Corn blight fungus. ANIMALS AND ANIMAL PARTS: a) Dust mite, b) Dandruff. GRASS AND WEED POLLEN: a) Daisy, b) Plantain, c) Gama grass, d) Ragweed, e) Ryegrass, f) Sedge. TREE POLLEN: a) Alder, b) Wattle, c) Beech, d) Birch, e) Ginko, f) Maple, g) Oak, h) Pine, i) Ash.

## Science Fair Ideas

- Most of the mineral grains you will observe in dust are quartz. Can you develop an easy examination technique to identify mineral grains in dust? Hint: Use polarized lighting (see Exploration 2.6) to determine if quartz is double refractive—if it bends polarized light (see "Lighting Techniques" in Appendix A).

- Design an experiment that lets you learn more about how dust settles. Are settling dust layers in a particular room type or space made of the same things—animal, vegetable, and mineral? Do all kitchens have the same type of dust, for example?

- Dandruff is a major component of dust. It is a common medical condition in which the scalp becomes dry and itchy resulting in the flaking of the top layer (i.e., the epidermis) of the skin. Make a wet mount of dandruff by rubbing your scalp and collecting falling skin cells in a drop of water on a microscope slide. Examine at 100X magnification. You may wish to make a stained preparation using methylene blue stain (see "Staining" in Appendix A). Can you observe any interior cell structures?

# Exploration 2.4

# Why Is Milk White?

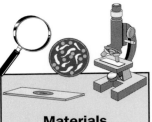

Whole milk is a mixture of particles. It contains 3 to 4 percent milk protein (casein), 4 to 5 percent fat, and approximately 4.5 percent milk sugar (lactose). The vast majority of the particles in milk are casein, which measure approximately 100 nm (nanometers) in diameter. (A nanometer is 1/1,000 of a micrometer or 1/1,000,000 of a millimeter.) The larger fat globules are 30 times larger—ranging in size from 3 to 15μm in diameter (see Figure 15).

### Materials

* glass
* homogenized whole milk
* whole milk—non-homogenized (from a dairy) if available, or homogenized heavy cream or condensed or evaporated milk
* eyedropper
* microscope slide
* coverslip
* compound microscope, with light source

Pour a glass of homogenized whole milk and observe if any of the milk protein particles settle out at the bottom of the glass. Your observations should confirm that milk is a mixture of small particles that are constantly in motion and that do not settle out upon standing. In short, milk is a colloid.

Try to get a sample of non-homogenized whole milk to study under the microscope. If you can't obtain non-homogenized milk, mix one part homogenized heavy cream, or condensed (or evaporated) milk, with 5 parts homogenized milk. Use an eyedropper to place a drop of this mixture on a microscope slide. Carefully add a coverslip. Observe the preparation carefully, beginning at medium (100X) magnification.

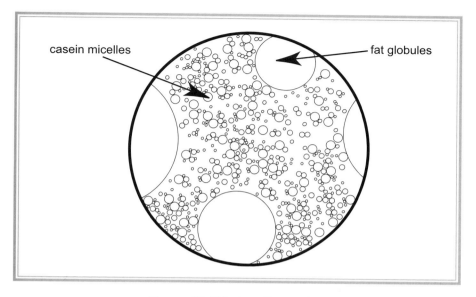

casein micelles

fat globules

**Figure 15.** Whole milk particles.

You may need to reduce the lighting by using the disc or iris diaphragm. Can you observe larger fat globules? Carefully focus in on one and switch to high power (430X) magnification. Increase the contrast by using the iris or disc diaphragm to reduce light in the field of view.

Can you measure the size of the observed fat globules? (See Exploration 1.8.) How are they different from the other observed particles? Can you also observe other, much smaller particles that appear in constant motion? These small particles are casein micelles—groups of the smaller casein particles. Watch them very closely. How far do individual micelles travel before they hit another particle? In whole milk, the casein micelles are so numerous that one can only travel about three times its diameter before it collides with another particle. Compare whole milk to condensed or evaporated milk under the microscope. Can you observe a greater number of casein micelles? How can you tell? *Hint:* Individual micelles will travel a shorter distance before a collision if they are more concentrated.

Both fat and casein particles do not allow light to pass through them but scatter it equally in all directions. Because there are so many of these particles, milk looks opaque or white.

## Science Fair Ideas

• Use the microscope to investigate the difference between homogenized and non-homogenized milk. Why is homogenization the preferred way of selling milk? *Hint:* Homogenization affects the size of fat globules.

• Can you use the microscope to detect mixed powdered milk from regular milk? Skim milk from whole milk?

• Use the microscope to find the components of soy milk. Is it a colloid? Does it have fat globules? Micelles?

• Explore Robert Brown's "active molecules"—tiny specks of moving matter. Make a wet mount of India ink. Observe this preparation at high (430X) magnification. Can you observe the endless flickering movement of the ink particles? Does milk show the same Brownian motion? Investigate other materials that are colloids: whipped cream, mayonnaise, and paint.

Exploration 2.5

# Why Are Pencils Hard or Soft?

## Materials

* paper punch
* index card, cut to 1 in x 3 in
* clear tape
* manual pencil sharpener
* wood pencils: hard and soft leads
* compound microscope, with light source
* white paper
* scissors
* 2 microscope slides

A pencil has a core of solid marking substance contained in a holder. The wooden pencil was invented in England in the mid-1500s. It used graphite (a crystalline form of carbon) to make its mark. The pencil was an improvement over the ancient Roman stylus, which was made of lead. Today we still call the core of a pencil the "lead" even though it is made from nontoxic graphite.

Graphite left a darker mark than lead, but it was so soft and brittle that it required a holder. At first, sticks of graphite were wrapped in string. Later, the graphite was inserted into wooden sticks that had been hollowed out by hand. The first mass-produced pencils were made in Nuremberg, Germany, in 1662. Today, powdered graphite, clay, and water are blended and made into small-diameter rods, dried, and heated to very high temperatures. Wax is added to give the rods smoothness. Varying the amount of clay determines the degree of hardness.

Wood for pencils must be straight-grained and of a texture that can be cut against the grain with a pencil sharpener. Cedar comes closest to these properties. About 98 percent of the wood used today in pencil manufacture comes from the incense cedar (*Calocedrus decurrens*) of western North America.

Construct several dry mount slides. Use a paper punch to punch a center hole in a piece of index card cut to 1 in x 3 in. Next, carefully place a piece of clear tape so that it covers the hole on the card. Turn the card over. The sticky surface will hold small solid objects.

Use a manual pencil sharpener to create graphite shavings that are allowed to fall onto the sticky surface of the dry mount. Create several dry mount preparations using pencil leads of various hardness. Be sure that each dry mount preparation is labeled.

Observe graphite shavings under medium (100X) and high dry (430X) magnification. Can you observe differences in the amount of clay added to make certain pencil leads harder? Make drawings of your observations.

Make pencil markings on white paper using various hardness pencil leads. Use scissors to cut out these markings and make press mounts of them. To make a press mount, place the cut-out paper on a clean microscope slide. Place another clean microscope slide on top of the sample, creating a sandwich. Examine the press mounts under medium (100X) magnification. Can you detect differences in pencil hardness? For example, can you observe differences in how individual paper fibers hold graphite from soft and hard pencil leads? Can you, like the famed consulting detective Sherlock Holmes, create a guide to pencil markings?

# Exploration 2.6

# The Mystery of the Glowing Crystal

**Materials**

* 2 polarizers
* compound microscope, with light source
* paper punch
* index card, cut to 1 in x 3 in
* clear tape
* specimen material: salt, sugar crystals, baking soda, and corn starch

Polarizing microscopy is a special lighting technique that forensic scientists use. They can identify fibers and certain materials based on their ability to bend light. This ability to bend light is called double refraction. Double-refracted materials appear to glow (i.e., show a pattern of colors) when viewed through polarizing filters. A polarizing filter allows only light rays that are oriented in the same direction (i.e., they are parallel) to pass through; light rays that are at other angles are screened out. That is why polarizing sunglasses are good at screening out certain light rays that cause glare.

Obtain polarizers by popping the lenses out of an inexpensive pair of polarizing sunglasses (or see supplier number 11 in Appendix B).

First, you must achieve crossed polarized light to view objects to determine if they are double refractive. Place one polarizer in the direct path of light before it passes through the specimen on the stage. Place the other polarizer on top of the eyepiece (see Figure 16). Carefully rotate the eyepiece polarizer (while looking through the eyepiece) until you obtain crossed polarized light. This will appear as a black field of view to your eye.

Now you can examine various fibers and materials to see if they are double refractive. To get started, make separate dry mounts of both salt and sugar crystals. Use a paper punch to punch a center hole in a 1-in x 3-in piece of index card. Next,

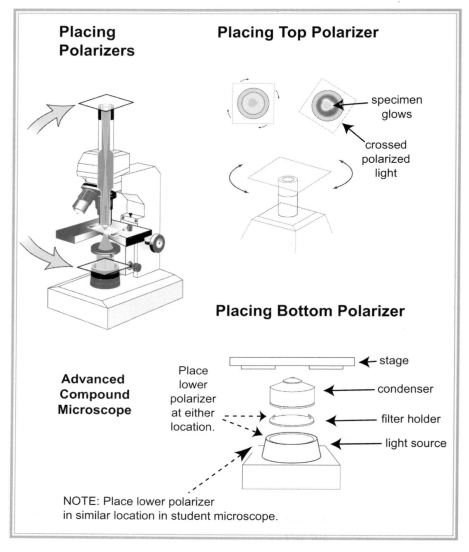

**Placing Polarizers**

**Placing Top Polarizer**

specimen glows

crossed polarized light

**Placing Bottom Polarizer**

**Advanced Compound Microscope**

Place lower polarizer at either location.

stage

condenser

filter holder

light source

NOTE: Place lower polarizer in similar location in student microscope.

**Figure 16.** Polarizing effect. Remember that the lower polarizer needs to be between the light source (or mirror) and the viewed object.

carefully place a piece of clear tape so that it covers the hole on the card. Turn the card over. The sticky surface will hold small solid objects. Carefully sprinkle salt and sugar crystals on separate dry mount slides.

Observe each dry mount separately under crossed polarized lighting, first at 100X, then at a higher (430X) magnification. Can you determine which of these two substances is double refractive?

Make dry mounts of other common chemical substances such as baking soda, cornstarch, and sugar substitutes. Record which substances are double refractive. Observe the substances that are double refractive. Are the glow colors unique or common to a particular substance?

## Science Fair Ideas

- Investigate whether particles of sand or marble are double refractive.

- Forensic scientists routinely use polarized lighting to identify polyester threads. Make permanent mounts of various natural and synthetic textile fiber types such as polyester, cotton, and wool. Are other synthetic fibers, like nylon, double refractive? What about silk?

- Allow drops of various solutions on clean microscope slides to evaporate (change from a liquid to a gas), leaving any solid crystals behind. For example, make a salt solution by mixing 1 to 3 teaspoons of salt and sugar in a glass of warm water. Stir to dissolve. Add drops of this solution to a clean microscope slide and allow the liquid to evaporate. Make a permanent mount and observe under medium (100X) magnification. Can you identify sugar and salt crystals? *Hint*: View your preparation under polarized light.

# Exploration 2.7

# How Do Toothpastes Work?

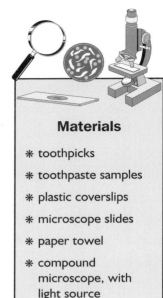

## Materials

* ✳ toothpicks
* ✳ toothpaste samples
* ✳ plastic coverslips
* ✳ microscope slides
* ✳ paper towel
* ✳ compound microscope, with light source

To be effective, a toothpaste must contain an abrasive material that removes the thin, adhesive film on teeth called plaque, yet not remove tooth enamel.

Use a toothpick to apply a small amount of a toothpaste sample to the center of a plastic coverslip. Apply the plastic coverslip containing the sample to the center of a clean glass microscope slide. Hold this preparation between your thumb and forefinger (see Figure 17). While applying gentle pressure with your thumb, rotate the coverslip with your thumb and index finger in a circular path approximately twenty times. Rinse the toothpaste off the coverslip and microscope slide under a faucet. Blot both items dry with a paper towel.

Place the prepared coverslip on the center of a different dry glass microscope slide. Examine the abrasion tracks under the medium magnification (100X) of a compound microscope. Characterize the type of abrasive(s) as polishing, light, or heavy. Use Figure 17c as a guide. Do some toothpastes use a combination of abrasives? In your notebook, make a table that summarizes and illustrates your findings.

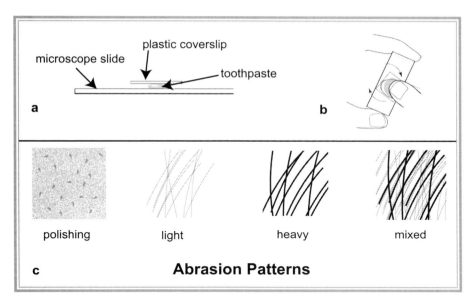

**Figure 17.** ABRASION PATTERN TEST. a) Side view of the microscope slide preparation. Remember to use a plastic coverslip. b) Performing the abrasion test. c) Abrasion patterns with "polishing," "light," and "heavy" abrasives. Remember, smaller-sized abrasive particles leave thinner abrasion pattern tracks.

## Science Fair Ideas

- Read toothpaste labels. Obtain toothpastes that contain carbonates, such as the mineral calcite (calcium carbonate—$CaCO_3$) and calcium phosphate (monetite, $CaHPO_4$). Observe lightly smeared toothpaste samples containing these ingredients under polarized light to see if this viewing method is of use in identifying toothpaste abrasives.

- Some toothpastes use sodium bicarbonate in their formulations. Examine toothpastes with this additive. Based upon your microscopic observations, is sodium bicarbonate an effective plaque fighter? Is it double refractive?

## Exploration 2.8

# What Are the Differences Between Synthetic and Natural Fibers?

**Materials**

* tweezers
* hair from various mammals and various synthetic fibers
* microscope slide
* eyedropper
* corn syrup
* coverslip
* pencil with eraser
* compound microscope, with light source
* clear tape
* scissors
* QX3 or other microscope with camera (optional)

Most forensic labs have trained microscopists who examine "trace evidence"—small particles—that includes hair and fibers.

Fibers obtained from plants or animals are known as natural fibers. Synthetic fibers are made from chemical-based raw materials that are squeezed out through tiny holes under pressure to form threads. Some synthetic fibers are nylon, polyester, and rayon.

Plant fibers come from the seed hairs, leaves and husks, and stems of the plant. The soft (bast) fibers from stems are primarily used in weaving textiles. The coarser (cordage) fibers from leaves and husks (outer seed coverings) are used for rope and twine. Animal fibers are provided, generally, by animal hair. In the case of silk, they come from the secretion of the silkworm. Use Table 2 as a guide to help you identify natural and synthetic fibers.

Being able to identify fibers is critical to your success as a microscopist. Create your own "reference fiber library" by

| Table 2. Guide To Natural and Synthetic Fibers | | |
| --- | --- | --- |
| **ANIMAL** | | |
| Human | | FIBER: Cylindrical<br><br>USE: Wigs |
| Wool | | FIBER: Cylindrical, coiled<br><br>USE: Textiles; carpets |
| Silk<br>cultivated<br>silkworm<br>*Bombyx mori* | | FIBER: Strongest of all natural fibers<br><br>USE: Textiles |
| **PLANT** | | |
| Cotton<br>*Gossypium*<br>species | | FIBER: Spiral twist; only natural fiber that has elasticity<br>USE: Textiles; thread; twine; paper |
| Flax<br>*Linum*<br>*usitatissimum* | | FIBER: Cylindrical, long and hollow<br><br>USE: Table linens, clothing |

| SYNTHETIC | | |
|---|---|---|
| Rayon | | FIBER: Extruded filament<br><br>USE: Clothing fabrics (long filament—triacetate rayon); filling materials in pillows, mattress pads, quilts; filtering agents in cigarettes (short filament—acetate rayon) |
| Nylon | | FIBER: Stretched or extruded; elastic filament<br><br>USE: Carpeting, clothing |
| Polyester | | FIBER: Stretched; hollow<br>USE: Lightweight clothing; insulation; water and wind-resistant fabrics |

preparing permanent mounts of collected fibers. A good place to begin is by visiting a local barbershop, hair salon, or pet-grooming shop and asking permission to collect hair samples. Expand your collection of animal hairs by including hamster, guinea pig, and gerbil hair types. Use Table 2 to help determine if a fiber is synthetic or natural.

To make a permanent mount, use tweezers to place a hair on a clean microscope slide. Then place a drop of corn syrup over the hair. Add a coverslip on top of the drop and use the eraser end of a pencil to press it gently down onto the slide. Examine the preparation first under scanning (40X), then medium (100X) magnification. Reduce lighting to obtain maximum contrast.

At crime scenes, evidence technicians use clear sticky tape to pick up fiber evidence. Try collecting fibers from various surfaces and clothing using this technique. As soon as you have lifted fibers off a surface, press the tape onto a clean microscope slide, pinning the fiber(s) to its surface. You may need scissors to trim off the ends of the tape. Examine a prepared fiber first under scanning (40X), then medium (100X) magnification. Reduce lighting to obtain maximum contrast. Can you identify natural and synthetic fiber types? Particular kinds of fibers?

Always record your notes and analysis results in your laboratory notebook. Careful and complete information is all-important to practicing forensic science—the methods of detecting criminal acts. If possible, use a camera attached to the microscope to make a photographic record of your microscopic observations. If available, use the QX3 digital computer microscope (see Appendix A) to take pictures of viewed samples.

Here are some additional fiber and hair explorations you can do.

## Identifying Floor Covering and Apparel Fibers

Investigate just what types of fiber (synthetic or natural) are used in carpeting. Study and compare individual fibers from at least five carpet types such as area rugs, wall-to-wall carpeting, and interior floor mats. Create a reference collection of fiber types. You might need to visit a carpet store and ask for samples.

## What Grade Is Wool?

Wool fiber comes in many grades or sizes. Fiber diameter determines its grade: fine (17–22μm), medium (22–30μm), coarse (31–36μm), and very coarse (36–40μm). Visit a fabric store and ask for samples of various wool fabrics. The grade information is usually contained on the product label. Make permanent mounts of single wool fibers and examine at 40X magnification. Can you identify various grades? Do your microscopic observations agree with the manufacturers' specifications?

## Whose Hair Is It?

Hairs are thin growths that protrude like filaments from the top skin layer, or epidermis, of mammals. The hair is composed of three layers. The outermost is the cuticle, which is made up of thin overlapping cells like shingles. Underneath the cuticle is the cortex, made of many elongated cells. In the center of the hair is the medulla, with its rectangular cells. Use Figure 19 as a guide to animal hairs. Visit these locations to obtain various hair samples: a barbershop, hair salon, and a pet-grooming shop.

Microscopists determine the medullary index of hair—the diameter of the medulla divided by the diameter of the hair. For example, humans have an index of less than 1/3 or 0.33. All other animal hair has a medullary index of greater than 0.50. Calculate the medullary index to determine whether a particular hair is human or animal.

### Science Fair Ideas

- Create a reference collection of various hairs. Ask your friends to submit unknown samples for you to identify.

- Conduct an experiment that demonstrates Locard's Principle—"every contact leaves a trace." Wash a T-shirt to remove any stray fibers. Dry the shirt alone. Put

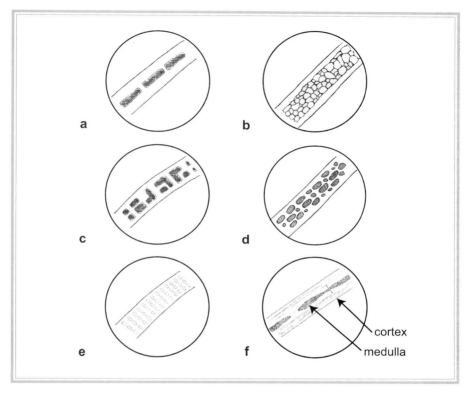

**Figure 19.** ANIMAL HAIRS: a) Cat, b) Deer, c) Dog, d) Rabbit, e) Mouse, f) Human.

on the shirt and conduct various exercises: rolling on a carpet, roughhousing with a friend, playing with your dog or cat. Remove the shirt and see if you can recover physical evidence—left-behind fibers—of these various contacts. Can you match the fibers collected from the shirt to other, similar fibers at each recorded scene?

• Once you are proficient at collecting fiber evidence at home, ask a friend to conduct similar "trace-leaving" exercises at his or her house. See if you can forensically trace your friend's journey. How good are you at evidence recovery?

## Chapter 3

# Just What Is a Microbe, Anyway?

### Antoni van Leeuwenhoek (1632–1723)

A microbe is a small organism of interest to someone. A Dutch cloth merchant, Antoni van Leeuwenhoek, was the first explorer of the living microscopic world, a micronaturalist. His illustrated letters to the Royal Society in London described microbes—bacteria, protozoa, and a variety of other, larger microlife-forms such as hydras and water fleas.

In this chapter you will explore various places where microbes dwell—their microhabitats—to better understand just what a microbe is.

Replica of van Leeuwenhoek's microscope

# Exploration 3.1

# What Bacteria Are in Your Mouth?

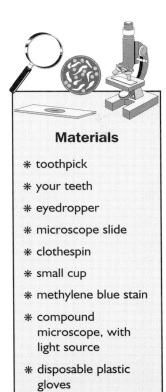

**Materials**

* toothpick
* your teeth
* eyedropper
* microscope slide
* clothespin
* small cup
* methylene blue stain
* compound microscope, with light source
* disposable plastic gloves
* safety goggles

Safety: Use care when working with biological stains. Avoid skin and eye contact. Wear eye and hand protection.

> Tho my teeth are kept unusually very clean, nevertheless when I view them in a Magnifying Glass, I find growing between them a little white matter as thick as wetted flower: in this substance tho I do not perceive any motion, I judged there might probably be live creatures.

*Antoni van Leeuwenhoek*
*September 17, 1683*

A biofilm is a community or a group of microorganisms attached to a solid surface. A biofilm community can include bacteria, fungi, yeasts, protozoa, and other microorganisms.

As did van Leeuwenhoek, you have certainly encountered biofilm on a regular basis. The plaque that forms on your teeth and causes tooth decay is a type of bacterial biofilm. The gunk that clogs your drains is also biofilm. If you have ever walked in a stream or river, you may have slipped on the biofilm-coated rocks.

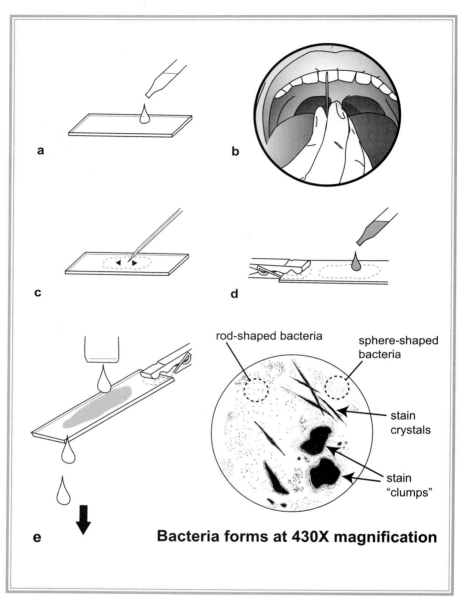

rod-shaped bacteria

sphere-shaped bacteria

stain crystals

stain "clumps"

**Bacteria forms at 430X magnification**

**Figure 20.** MAKING A STAINED SMEAR. a) Add a drop of water. b) Use a toothpick to scrape plaque from your teeth. c) Mix teeth scrapings in the water drop and allow to dry. d) Add a drop or two of stain; wait 2 to 3 minutes. e) Gently wash using drops of water. Allow to air dry again.

Protein is why biofilms form. Protein is the glue substance in nature. As protein adheres to a surface, it flattens and forms a thin, tight glue layer to which microbes, protozoa, and invertebrates will attach.

Investigate the plaque biofilm community by using a toothpick to scrape and remove plaque from your teeth. Is it like van Leeuwenhoek described? Use Figure 20 as a guide in making a stained smear. Mix the collected plaque with a drop of water on a microscope slide. Allow the drop to air dry. Use a clothespin to hold the slide over a cup. Collect some methylene blue stain with an eyedropper and "flood" the smear on the slide by allowing drops to pile up creating a single large drop. Let the stain act for 2 to 3 minutes. Use another eyedropper to apply single drops of water to rinse the stain off the slide. Allow the slide to air dry. Examine the slide under 430X (or a higher magnification if you can). What are the main types of bacteria in your mouth—rods or spheres?

Can you estimate the size of these mouth microbes? (See Exploration 1.8.) Record your observations in your notebook, including drawings of biofilm plaque bacteria. Use Figure 21 as a guide in identifying biofilm microbes.

## Science Fair Ideas

- Sample biofilms in the wild by making wet mounts of scrapings from various microhabitats: aquarium filter material and tank glass films, submerged rocks, and the common green coverings of the alga *Protococcus*, on trees. Use Figure 21 as a guide in identifying biofilm microbes. Examine your wet mount preparations under both medium (100X) and high-power (430X) magnification of a compound microscope.

- Use plastic coverslips or small pieces of clear or colored

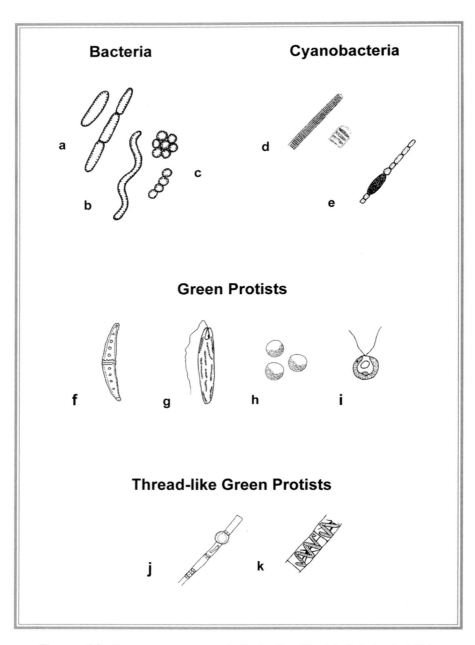

**Figure 21.** Biofilm microbes: a) Rods (bacilli), b) Spirals (spirilla), c) Spheres (cocci), d) *Oscillatoria*, e) *Anabaena*, f) *Closterium*, g) *Euglena*, h) *Protococcus*, i) *Chlamydomonas*, j) *Oedogonium*, k) *Spirogyra*.

acetate sheets as "microbe traps." You can use plastic clothespins to hold these traps. Tie the clothespins together on a string (knotted at 12-in intervals) to create a "trap string." This string of traps can be set either vertically or horizontally by attaching it to a series of floats. Use Figure 22 as a guide in setting and examining these traps. Try setting traps in an aquarium, pond, or gutter full of rainwater. For example, you may want to investigate whether color affects biofilm formation. Wait 2 to 3 weeks (or longer), then examine the biofilm as a wet mount at 40X to 430X magnification.

- Investigate soil biofilms by burying microscope slides into topsoils for extended time periods. For example, do special biofilm populations emerge under fruit trees in orchards during the fall? Does the application of fertilizers or pesticides affect biofilm populations in the topsoil? Do subsoils support the same biofilms as topsoils? After 4 to 6 weeks, carefully dig up the slides, wipe one side off with a paper towel, and add methylene blue or crystal violet stain, dropwise, to the other, soil covered, side. Let the stain act for 2 to 3 minutes. Use another eyedropper to apply single drops of water to rinse the stain off the slide. Allow the slide to air dry. Examine the stained soil slide under 430X (or higher) magnification. Use Figure 21 as a guide to soil microbes.

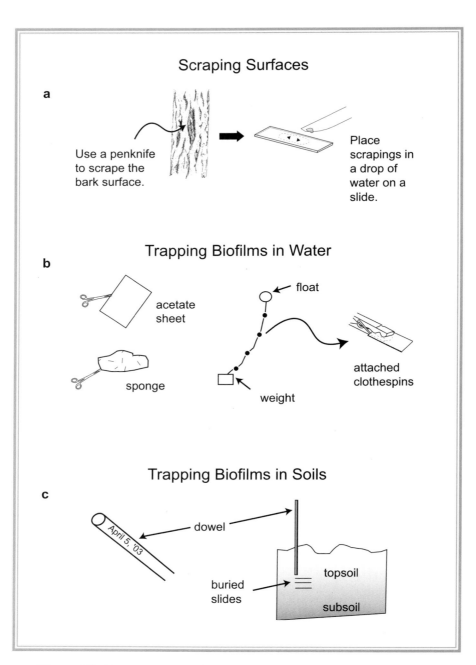

**Figure 22.** MICROLIFE TRAPS: a) Scraping surfaces. b) Trapping biofilms in water. c) Trapping biofilms in soils.

# What Microbes Do You Eat?

**Safety:** Use care when working with biological stains. Avoid skin and eye contact. Wear eye and hand protection.

Yogurt is a semi-solid milk product that originated centuries ago in Bulgaria. To make yogurt, milk is boiled to concentrate the milk solids. Then the solids are mixed with cultures of *Lactobacillus bulgaricus* and *Streptococcus lactis*. The mixture is then heated to about 45 degrees Celsius (113 degrees Fahrenheit) until the lactic acid content, produced by the bacteria, reaches levels high enough to solidify the milk solids.

## Materials

* 2 eyedroppers
* microscope slide
* toothpick
* yogurt having active cultures and other yogurt products
* wooden clothespin
* small cup
* methylene blue stain
* corn syrup
* coverslip
* pencil with eraser
* compound microscope, with light source
* disposable plastic gloves
* safety goggles

Use a toothpick to gather a small amount of yogurt for a stained smear preparation that will be examined under a compound microscope.

Place a drop of water on a clean microscope slide using an eyedropper. Use the flat portion of a toothpick to pick up some yogurt. Mix the yogurt on the toothpick in the water drop to create a thin smear in the middle portion of the slide. Discard the toothpick. Allow the smear to air dry.

Use Figure 20 as a guide to making a stained smear. Use a wooden clothespin to hold the slide. Hold the slide over a cup. Collect some methylene blue stain with an eyedropper and "flood" the smeared area of the slide by allowing drops to pile up creating a single, large drop. Let the stain act for 2 to 3 minutes. Use another eyedropper to apply single drops of water to rinse the stain off the slide. Allow the slide to air dry. Use another eyedropper to add a pea-size drop of corn syrup to the stained area, and then add a coverslip. Use the eraser end of a pencil to press the coverslip down over the smear area. Wash your hands thoroughly.

In identifying yogurt bacteria, you should know that *Lactobacillus* is rod-shaped and *Streptococcus* is spherical. Sample and microscopically examine different yogurt products. Do all of them contain bacteria? Which ones?

## Science Fair Ideas

- There are a number of milk products broken down by microbes (i.e., they are fermented) that you can examine. Make smear stain preparations of the following foods. Do all contain the same type of bacteria—rods and spheres?

    –cultured buttermilk

    –acidophilus milk

    –sour cream

    –kefir

    –koumiss

- The great biologist Louis Pasteur (1822–1895) found that heating milk over a period of time kills certain bacteria that cause disease. This process—pasteurization—is now routinely used on a variety of foods, including milk. Obtain a fresh, unopened, carton of pasteurized milk. In your notebook, record the purchase date, the expiration date, and the temperature of your refrigerator. Pour out a small sample from the carton. Like commercial labs that test milk, make a methylene blue test of this milk sample by examining a methylene-blue-stained smear of a drop of the sample mixed with a drop of water on a clean microscope slide. Allow this mixture to dry before and after you stain it with methylene blue. Can you observe any bacteria? Use Figure 20 as a guide for staining. Does pasteurization kill all bacteria? **With your parent's permission**, take samples from the milk carton stored in a refrigerator over a 2- to 3-week period, and at least 1 week after the expiration date (don't drink from this carton). Do you observe increasing numbers of bacteria in your smear preparations? Read up on the process of pasteurization. Today, many health authorities want all apple cider to be pasteurized. From your microscopic observations on milk, why would this be a good idea?

• During the process of yogurt making, certain milk bacteria produce lactic acid, which solidifies the milk. Design an experiment that investigates if these same types of bacteria are responsible for the souring of milk or turning of cream.

# Exploration 3.3

## How Do Decomposers Do Their Work?

**Safety:** Use care when working with biological stains. Avoid skin and eye contact. Wear eye and hand protection.

Some microbes are decomposers—microorganisms such as bacteria and fungi (molds) that obtain their food by breaking down the nutrients in dead organisms or animal wastes. Figure 23 illustrates some common decomposers.

Molds reproduce by releasing spores—microscopic bodies carried in the air. When spores land on a new surface, they germinate and grow slender tubes called hyphae. The hyphae of some molds

### Materials

* bread, without preservatives
* margarine or whipped topping container, with lid
* teaspoon
* nail
* magnifying glass
* toothpick
* iodine stain
* eyedropper
* microscope slide
* plastic coverslip
* compound microscope, with light source
* disposable plastic gloves
* safety goggles

(deuteromycetes) have "tube dividers" or cross walls, while the hyphae of other molds (zygomycetes) lack cross walls. Cross walls control the flow of cytoplasm within hyphae. A cottony mass of tangled hyphae, called the mycelium, makes up the body of a fungus.

Before a mold can reproduce, a fruiting body—a slender stalk supporting a spore case containing thousands of spores—must grow up from the hyphae. Each fungal spore is capable

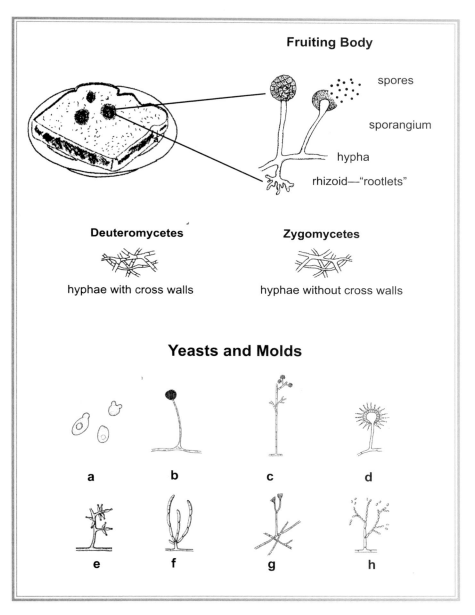

**Figure 23.** The fruiting body of a mold makes spores. When spores germinate on a surface, they make hyphae. Deuteromycete molds have cross walls on their hyphae; zygomycetes do not. DECOMPOSER: a) Yeast (*Saccharomyces*). MOLDS: b) *Mucor*, c) *Botrytis*, d) *Aspergillus*, e) *Trichoderma*, f) *Fusarium*, g) *Penicillium*, h) *Neurospora*.

of producing an entire mycelium. A mycelium will grow on virtually anything from which the fungus can obtain food. A single fungus can produce more than a half mile of hyphae in just four hours.

A slice of bread (especially one made without preservatives) can become a place for many microbes—especially molds—to grow. Create a moisture chamber by placing a slice of bread on the inside lid of a margarine or whipped topping container and sprinkle 1 to 2 teaspoons of water on the bread. Use the point of a nail to punch several holes in the bottom of the container and place it upside down on the lid. Observe the contents of the container daily with a magnifying glass. Once you can detect mold on the bread, use a clean toothpick to gather a small amount the of cottony material (hyphae) and mix it with a drop of iodine stain on a microscope slide. Add a coverslip and observe under 100X magnification of a compound microscope. Use Figure 23 as a guide in helping you identify a particular mold microbe. Look for spore cases and study hyphae for cross walls. Is your mold a deuteromycete or a zygomycete—does it have cross walls or not? Record your observations, including drawings, in your notebook.

## Science Fair Ideas

- Use a dry cotton swab to capture any mold spores that may be present on various surfaces, such as fruits, vegetables, bark, and plant stems. Transfer these spores to a new bread slice (inoculate them) by gently rubbing the swab onto the surface of the bread. Place the bread slice in the moisture chamber. Again observe the bread surface daily with a magnifying glass for signs of mold growth. Make drawings of the fruiting bodies and compare them to those in Figure 23.

- Obtain a piece of molding fruit and a similar fruit without any signs of mold. Wet one end of a toothpick. Use this wetted surface to collect mold spores from the surface of the moldy piece of fruit. Use the toothpick as an "inoculating needle" to inoculate (transfer) mold spores to the piece of nonmoldy fruit by breaking its skin surface. Place the fruit in a location where you can observe it with a magnifying glass over time—about 2 to 3 weeks. If available, use the QX3 microscope to create a time-lapse movie of the growing mold.

- Place pieces of rotting wood or decaying leaves inside a moisture chamber to provide an ideal environment for mold growth. Which material has the greatest number of different molds? Do different molds appear over time?

## Exploration 3.4

# Looking at Pond-Life "Animacules"

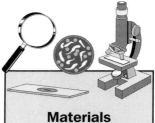

**Materials**

* ✳ kitchen baster
* ✳ pond, puddle, or aquarium
* ✳ collection jar
* ✳ eyedropper
* ✳ microscope slide
* ✳ plastic coverslip
* ✳ modeling clay or silicone culture gum
* ✳ compound microscope, with light source

"I looked at it [pond water] through a microscope and I discovered in this water so unbelievably many little animacules."

*Antoni van Leeuwenhoek*
*June 28, 1713*

See if you can use van Leeuwenhoek's own descriptions (see Table 3, p. 78) in identifying various pond microbes.

Use a kitchen baster to gather water samples from a pond or puddle—or even from an aquarium. Transfer water samples, including some bottom muds, to a collection jar. Also collect small floating and submerged aquatic plants or bits of submerged leaves and plant matter. Cover the jar to prevent evaporation, and keep it on a sunny windowsill.

Use an eyedropper to sample the jar at various levels of the jar—bottom, middle, and top. Make wet mount preparations by placing a drop of collected water on a clean microscope slide. Carefully lower the coverslip over the drop so that it spreads evenly without creating air bubbles.

Also try constructing a micro aquarium—useful for observing larger microlife-forms that are attached to small pieces of aquatic plants. Roll a piece of modeling clay or silicone culture gum into a thin rod that is approximately 2.5 cm (1 in) long. Silicone culture gum is an inexpensive material that allows oxygen to pass into the well's interior to prolong organism viability for days. (See suppliers 1 and 11 in Appendix B.) Carefully shape this strip into a circle in the center of a clean microscope slide. To avoid leaks, be sure to press down so that the clay and the glass form a tight seal. Using an eyedropper, fill the area inside the clay circle (the micro aquarium pocket) with your sample. Make sure that no air bubbles are formed when the coverslip is added. Use Figure 24 as a guide to making a micro aquarium and Table 3 to identify pond microbes.

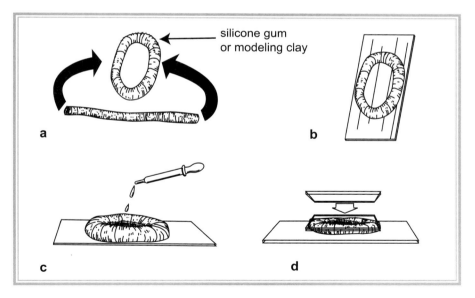

**Figure 24.** Micro aquaria and microbes. a) Roll silicone culture gum or clay into a thin rod. b) Form a well on a clean microscope slide; be sure to press down to make a tight seal. c) Use an eyedropper to add a water sample. Continue to add drops until almost overflowing. d) Carefully add a coverslip; avoid creating air pockets.

| Table 3. Van Leeuwenhoek's Microbe Descriptions ||
| Description | Hint |
| --- | --- |
| "A much bigger sort of animal . . . would let down their horns so far you would think, on seeing them through the microscope, that they were several fathoms long." | "Horns" are tentacles. |
| "I paid great attention to their revolving toothed wheelwork; I saw incredibly great motion. . . ." | describing "wheel" animacules |
| "I saw a floating . . . a great many green round particles, of the bigness of sand grains." | large ball-shaped colony |
| "In structure these little animals were fashioned like a bell, and at the round opening they made such a stir . . . I must have seen quite 20 of these little animals on their long tails . . . yet in an instant, as it were, they pulled in their bodies and tails together. . . ." | describing a ciliate on a stalk |

## Science Fair Ideas

- Use the QX3 computer microscope to take pictures of organisms that illustrate van Leeuwenhoek's descriptions.

- Create a "microhabitat list" of places where these micro-life-forms are found—e.g., edge of a pond, on the roots of the floating plant duckweed, etc.

# Chapter 4

# *The Secret Lives of Plants*

## William Withering (1741–1799)

The man credited with introducing the plant-derived drug digitalis into medicine for treating heart disease in humans was the botanist and physician William Withering. He is also known for inventing the "pocket" or "box" microscope, which featured a single low-power lens mounted over a small stage. The entire instrument—5X lens, brass lens holder, specimen stage, and support rod—fit neatly into a small rectangular wooden box.

Without the microscope, our knowledge of plants would be very sketchy. In this chapter you will explore how plants grow, what chemicals they make, and how they recycle gases, converting carbon dioxide into oxygen.

Withering's Botanical Microscope

## Exploration 4.1

# How Do Roots Grow?

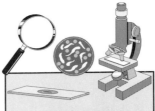

Safety: Use care when working with biological stains. Avoid skin and eye contact. Wear eye and hand protection.

Roots anchor plants in the ground. They help absorb and transport water and nutrients. They also serve as storage organs.

Plants grow when cells in special areas of the plant, called growth zones or meristems, divide. Two main growth areas in plants are located at the tips of their roots and shoots.

If possible, view a prepared microscope slide of an onion root tip. Ask your science teacher if you can borrow one. View the stained slide at medium (100X) magnification. Use Figure 25 as a guide to root anatomy. See if you can find the following structures and regions on the slide: root cap, growing tip (meristem region), region of cell elongation, and region of mature root cells with root hairs.

### Materials

* prepared microscope slide of onion root tip (longitudinal section)
* compound microscope, with light source
* onion or garlic bulb
* toothpicks
* small glass
* fine scissors
* ruler
* small paper cup
* tweezers
* microscope slide
* an adult
* single-edge razor blade
* eyedropper
* iodine stain
* plastic coverslip
* paper towel
* pencil with eraser
* disposable plastic gloves
* safety goggles

You can investigate this growth zone by making a squash preparation of an onion root tip. To grow onion tips, select a small onion or garlic clove. Insert toothpicks so that the bulb is suspended in a small glass container. Add water so that the bottom third is submerged. Make sure you put the root end in the water. Watch for the appearance of root tips in about a week. Use fine scissors to cut root tips that are about 5 to 10 mm (0.5 to 1 cm) in length. Place them in a small paper cup containing water. Use tweezers to place a cut root tip in the center of a clean microscope slide. **Ask an adult** to use a

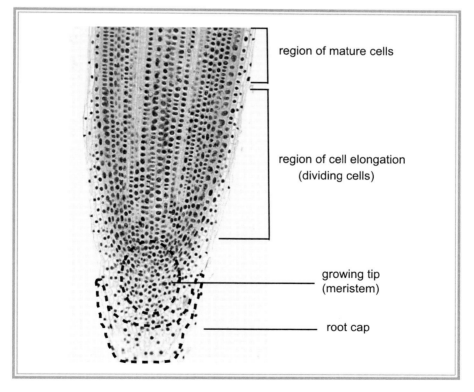

**Figure 25.** ONION ROOT TIP. Look closely in the region of cell elongation. Can you detect dividing cells?

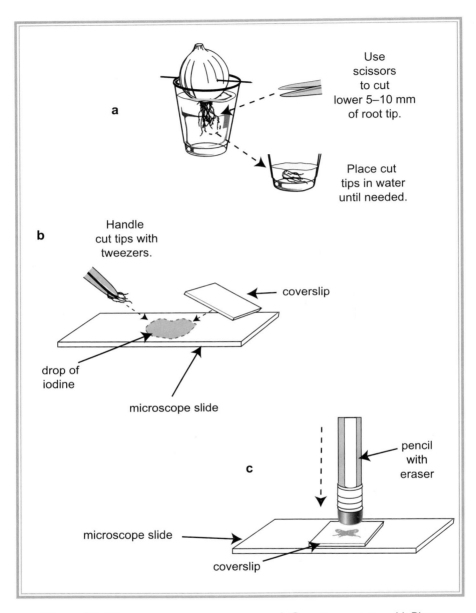

**Figure 26.** MAKING A SQUASH PREPARATION. a) Growing root tips. b) Place cut tips in stain; add a coverslip. c) Carefully use a pencil eraser tip to squash the cut tips. Under scanning (40X) magnification, look at the edges of squashed tissue. Observe groups of single cells at 100X–430X magnification.

single-edge razor blade to cut away all but the bottom 2 mm of the root tip.

Use Figure 26 as a guide in making squash preparations. First, use an eyedropper to add 3 drops of water over the root tip. Add a drop of iodine stain. Continue to add drops of iodine, as needed, until the tissue is stained—i.e., it is light brown. Place a plastic coverslip on top of the plant tissue. Use a paper towel to wipe up any excess liquid outside the coverslip. Position the eraser end of a pencil on top of the root tip under the coverslip. Carefully apply a small amount of pressure, and at the same time give the pencil a slight twist, to squash and spread the tissues. Make sure that the plant tissues are separated; if not, repeat the squash procedure.

View your prepared slide at medium (100X) magnification. Focus on individual cells. Switch to a high dry (430X) magnification and see if you can identify cells that are dividing. Use Figure 25 as a guide to dividing plant cells.

## Science Fair Idea

Scientists have found that cell division occurs around noon in many plants. Confirm this conclusion by designing some experiments using onion root tips. What about the effect of daylight savings time? Do plants reset their biological clocks?

Exploration 4.2

# How Do Leaves Breathe?

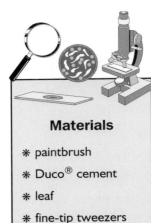

**Materials**

* paintbrush
* Duco® cement
* leaf
* fine-tip tweezers
* microscope slide
* plastic coverslip
* compound microscope, with light source

Openings in leaves are called stomata. They allow the movement of gases (oxygen and carbon dioxide) and water vapor during photosynthesis.

You can make impressions of the outer leaf surfaces to visualize these tiny openings. Use a paintbrush to apply a thin layer of Duco® cement to a leaf's surface (above or below). After the cement dries, use tweezers to carefully peel away the thin layer of dried cement from the leaf.

Make permanent mount preparations of leaf casts by placing the film on a microscope slide. Use Figure 27 as a guide. Examine your slides first under scanning (40X), then medium (100X) magnification. How many stomata does a leaf have in a 1-square-cm area? Is this number the same for a particular type of plant, or does it change?

*Note:* You could use a metric ruler to measure and mark a 1-sq-cm area to cast. The area of the field of view at 40X magnification is 12.5 sq mm; at 100X it is 2 sq mm.

## Science Fair Ideas

• Are stomata more numerous on the bottom or top surfaces of leaves?

• Could you use the number of stomata in leaves to identify

different types of plants—monocots and dicots? Leaves of monocots have parallel veins, while dicot leaves have veins that look like a criss-crossed network.

• Do desert plants such as cacti have larger numbers of stomata than non-desert or tropical plants? *Note:* Place cement on areas between spines.

• Do plants keep stomata open longer in very wet conditions, or in periods of drought?

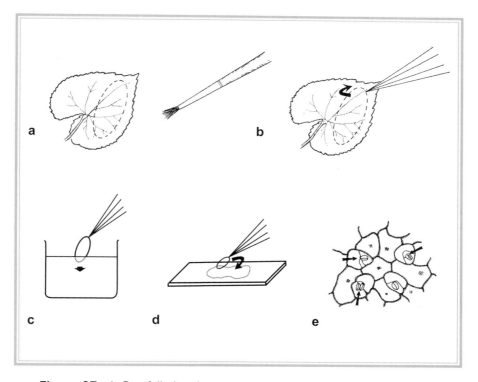

**Figure 27.** a) Carefully brush on cement over an area on the upper or bottom surface of a leaf. Allow the cement to dry. b) Use fine tweezers to remove the dried cement casting. c) Dip the cement casting in water to allow it to unfold. d) Carefully drop the leaf casting onto a drop of water on a clean microscope slide. Add coverslip. e) Observe stomata in leaf casts at medium (100X) magnification.

## Exploration 4.3

# What Is the Pollen Index?

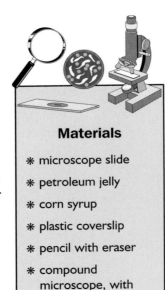

### Materials

* microscope slide
* petroleum jelly
* corn syrup
* plastic coverslip
* pencil with eraser
* compound microscope, with light source

Pollen consists of tiny grains that are produced in the male organs of flowering and cone-bearing plants. Many people are allergic to pollen. Large amounts of pollen in the air can cause allergic individuals to develop hay fever, asthma, and other allergic symptoms.

To better inform people who are sensitive to various pollen and mold allergens (a substance that brings about an allergic response), the American Academy of Allergy, Asthma and Immunology has developed an index that relates pollen and mold spore counts to an index of potential allergic response.

Using your finger, coat the center one-third of a clean microscope slide with a *thin layer* of petroleum jelly. An area of one square inch is fine—a typical glass slide measures 1 in x 3 in. Place the coated slide in an outside location so that it can pick up pollen from the air. Choose a location that is exposed to uninterrupted natural air currents, not drafts or air movements created by fans or vehicles.

After a twenty-four-hour period, bring the slide inside and add 2 to 3 drops of corn syrup. Apply a coverslip over the coated area. Use the eraser end of a pencil to press it down onto the slide surface to get a good seal. Use Figure 14 as a guide to identifying pollen types—tree, grass, and weed—and molds. Record your pollen calculations and counts by date in your notebook.

You may choose to prepare a "total" pollen count (all pollen types) or limit your count report to a particular pollen type. Calculate the pollen count as follows:

1. Calculate the diameter of one field of view—see Exploration 1.8 and Table 1.

2. Count the number of pollen grains in several fields of view (at least five). Obtain the average number of pollen grains (ANPG) per field by dividing the total number of pollen grains counted by the number of fields viewed. For example: A total of 9 pollen grains were counted in 10 individual fields.

$$\text{ANPG} = 9 \div 10 = 0.9 \text{ pollen grains}$$

3. Multiply the average number of pollen grains (ANPG) by the width of the coverslip (in millimeters) divided by the field diameter. Then multiply by 2 (a mathematical factor) to arrive at the pollen count. For example:

$$\frac{\text{ANPG x width of coverslip}}{\text{field diameter}} \times \text{factor} = \text{pollen count}$$

$$\frac{0.9 \text{ pollen grains x 22 mm}}{1.4 \text{ mm}} \times 2 = 28 \text{ pollen grains/coverslip}$$

4. Compare the pollen count to Table 4 to determine the pollen index.

| Table 4. Pollen Index | |
|---|---|
| **Index** | **Pollen Count** |
| Low | < 21 |
| Medium | 21–50 |
| High | 51–100 |
| Extreme | > 101 |

## Science Fair Ideas

- Compare your pollen index count to that reported by the National Weather Service, local television stations, or newspapers.

- In which months of the year do you see pollen counts rise and fall?

- Which pollen types occur with greatest frequency: tree, grasses, or weeds?

- Create a pollen reference collection by collecting pollen from plants and trees in the spring. Use the flat end of a toothpick to collect samples from anthers and male pinecones. Make permanent mounts of the collected samples. Use your reference collection to help you identify pollen index samples.

# Exploration 4.4

# Are All Starch Grains Alike?

Plants usually produce more sugars by photosynthesis than they can use. They convert this excess sugar to starch. Plants can store starch molecules in clusters or grains. Some plants, such as potatoes, store starch in modified underground stems called tubers—familiar as potatoes. Others, such as bananas, store starch in their fruit. Still others store starch in their seeds as is the case of the corn plant.

The starch grains from various plant sources each have a unique appearance. Let's examine starch grains from various plant sources.

## Materials

* toothpicks
* cornstarch
* microscope slides
* coverslips
* compound microscope, with light source
* an adult
* white potato, sweet potato, apple, banana
* wheat starch or wheat grains
* knife or single-edge razor blade
* tweezers
* eyedropper
* rice starch or rice grains

Wet a toothpick with water. Dip the wetted end into some cornstarch, purchased at a grocery store. Mix this small amount of cornstarch in a drop of water on a microscope slide. Make a wet mount by carefully lowering a coverslip over the drop so that it spreads evenly without creating air bubbles. Observe the preparation at low (40X) magnification under a compound microscope. Can you see any crevices? The cornstarch grain has a small, dark, central point with three or four radiating crevices.

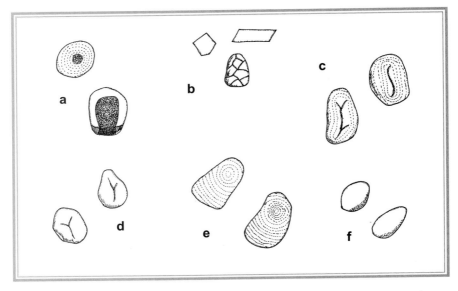

**Figure 28.** STARCH GRAINS: a) Tapioca starch, b) Rice starch, c) Bean starch, d) Cornstarch, e) Potato starch, f) Wheat starch.

Use Figure 28 as a guide in identifying starch grains. Most have a dark area called a hilum. This is the oldest part of the starch grain, around which additional starch is laid down over time.

**Ask an adult** to cut a potato in half. Use a toothpick to pick up a small amount of potato material and mix it in a drop of water on a microscope slide. Add a coverslip and observe under scanning (40X) magnification. Can you observe oval or transparent bodies that are shaped like clam shells? Can you observe a hilum and surrounding concentric rings called striations? Is the starch from a white potato similar to that from a sweet potato? Try sampling an apple. A banana. Can you detect starch grains?

Try to obtain wheat starch at your local grocery store. If a commercial source is unavailable, place some wheat grains in water for 24 hours to soften. **Ask an adult** to carefully slice a grain, lengthwise, using a knife or single-edge razor blade. Now pick up a half grain using tweezers and dip its cut end in a drop of water on a clean microscope slide. Examine these deposited starch grains at scanning (40X) magnification under a compound microscope. Use this same technique to examine rice starch grains.

## Science Fair Ideas

- Plant starches are sometimes used as adulterants—bulk materials used as filler in food products. The fillers cost less than the main ingredient itself, lowering overall manufacturing costs. Examine white flour, a food product consisting of ground wheat grain. Sometimes millers add or adulterate this food product with potato starch. Flour sometimes also contains impurities, such as the ground remains of various insects like mealworm larvae. Can you observe any adulterants or other contaminants in locally purchased white flour?

- Cocoa is another food product that is adulterated with other starch types. Can you identify them?

- Artificial honey is sometimes adulterated with starches, while pure honey will always have pollen grains. Make wet mounts of various commercial and locally produced (pure) honey samples, if possible. Can you detect starch adulterants? Use Figure 14 as a guide to pollen types.

- View potato and other starch grains under polarized light (see Appendix A). Do they bend light twice?

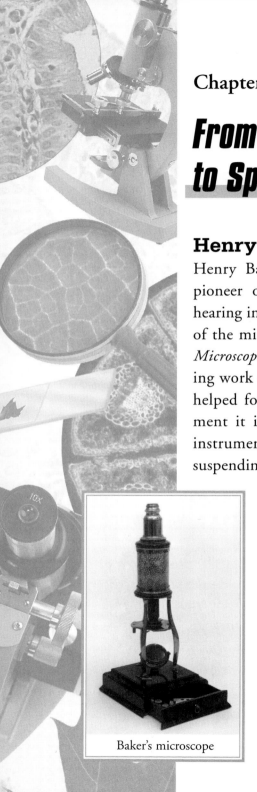

# Chapter 5

# From "Wheel Animals" to Spider's Silk

## Henry Baker (1698–1774)

Henry Baker was a naturalist, poet, and pioneer of education for the speech and hearing impaired. One of the first historians of the microscope, Henry Baker wrote *The Microscope Made Easy* in 1742. His pioneering work on the aquatic invertebrate *Hydra* helped form the microscope as the instrument it is today. Baker collaborated with instrument maker John Cuff (1708–1772), suspending a lens on a horizontal arm above a circular stage. Light was directed through a hole in the stage using a mirror mounted at the base.

Microscopes help us understand how cells work together to form tissues and organs—the stuff of which larger organisms are made. In this chapter you will use a microscope to answer questions about how animals age, how they obtain food, and how they make and use unique materials.

Baker's microscope

# Exploration 5.1

# How Small Is the Smallest Animal?

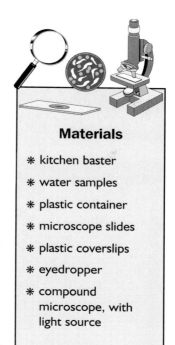

## Materials

* ✶ kitchen baster
* ✶ water samples
* ✶ plastic container
* ✶ microscope slides
* ✶ plastic coverslips
* ✶ eyedropper
* ✶ compound microscope, with light source

Rotifers, or "wheel animals," were first described in 1702 by the great microscopist Antoni van Leeuwenhoek in a letter to the Royal Society in London. His description, "two little wheels, which displayed a swift rotation," has given the name—wheel animals—to them ever since. They occur in an endless variety of microhabitats: ponds and puddles, between damp soil particles, and even on mosses.

There are quite a number of rotifers. Some are encased within sculptured shells; others look like miniature worms that inch along. Still others are master builders; attached to submerged objects or plants, they construct symmetrical tubes.

A common rotifer is *Philodina*, which is so abundant that almost any drop of water from a pond, ditch, or gutter will contain it. It resembles an inchworm with two rotating wheel organs.

Using a kitchen baster, collect outdoor water samples and place them in collecting containers. Try sampling from a variety of microhabitats: standing water in gutters, ditches, or ponds. Examine each water sample by making a wet mount. Use an eyedropper to sample the collection containers. Place a drop of water from each on clean microscope slides. Add

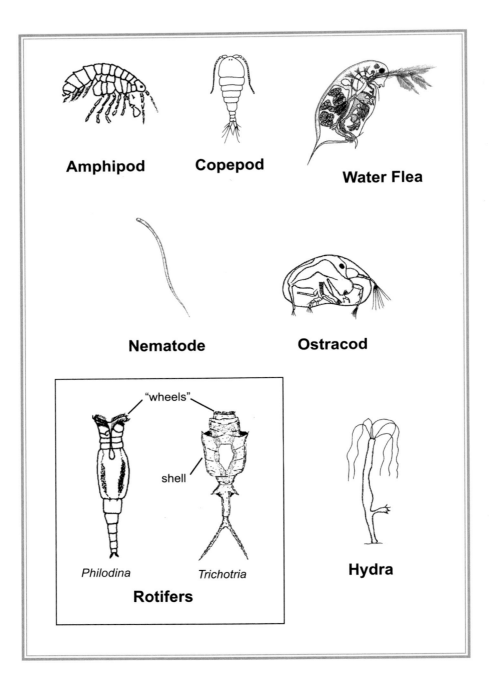

**Figure 29.** Micro animals.

coverslips and examine first under medium (100X) magnification. Use Figure 29 as a guide to rotifers and other micro animals. How many kinds can you identify?

Measure the size of a rotifer. Compare its size to that of other micro animals such as hydras, water fleas, and copepods. Which is the smallest animal?

## Science Fair Ideas

- Rotifers are also used as fish food, and pet stores usually have vials of dried *Brachionus* eggs for hatching. *Brachionus* ranges in size up to 300 $\mu$m—about 1/3 mm. Prepare a micro aquarium so that you can observe eggs develop and hatch. Place a small number of eggs in the sealed aquarium space and observe over time at low power (40X) magnification. Write a report on how the hatching process occurs.

- If you have a QX3 microscope, make movies illustrating rotifer wheel organs.

Exploration 5.2

# How Do Hydras Capture Their Prey?

Hydras are one of the few commonly observed freshwater coelenterates, or tentacle animals. They are usually plentiful in unpolluted still waters, where they attach to aquatic vegetation, fallen leaves, and submerged stones.

Hydras have five to eight tentacles that vary in length from species to species. They range from colorless to brown; some are even green due to the presence of tiny green protists that live within their bodies.

**Under adult supervision**, gather submerged vegetation from unpolluted ponds and other locations. Place it in a jar or shallow pan. Overnight, visible hydras will come to the surface where they can be picked up using an eyedropper. Sometimes it is easier just to transfer a hydra that is clinging to a small piece of material.

Place hydras in a micro aquarium. To construct one, roll a piece of modeling clay or silicone culture gum into a thin rod that is approximately 2.5 cm (1 in) long. Silicone culture gum is an inexpensive material that allows oxygen to pass into the well's interior to prolong organism viability for days (see suppliers 1 and 11 in Appendix B). Carefully shape this strip into a circle in the center of a clean microscope slide. To avoid

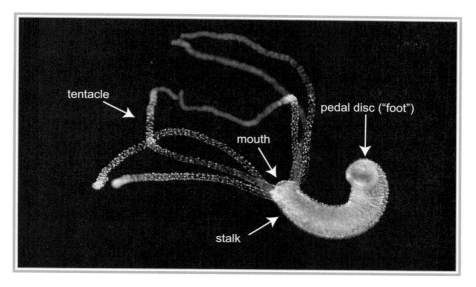

**Figure 30.** Hydra anatomy.

leaks, be sure to press down so that the clay and the glass form a tight seal. Using an eyedropper, fill the area inside the micro aquarium pocket with your sample. Make sure that no air bubbles are formed when the coverslip is added (see Figure 24).

Place the micro aquarium on the stage and allow the hydra to relax and extend. Using scanning (40X) magnification, observe the body plan of a hydra—a crown of 5 to 8 tentacles atop a long, flexible column. The tentacles contain stinging cells called nematocysts; these surround a mouth that is capable of capturing prey. Hydras uses their nematocysts as miniature syringes, injecting a numbing poison into any micro crustacean unlucky enough to brush against its tentacles (see Figure 30).

## Science Fair Idea

If you have a QX3 microscope; make a movie illustrating how a hydra feeds.

# Exploration 5.3

## How Do Feathers Maintain Their Shape?

### Materials

* a feather
* magnifying glass, 5X or 10X
* scissors
* microscope slide
* eyedropper
* corn syrup
* plastic coverslip
* pencil with eraser
* compound microscope, with light source

Feathers help birds fly, and they also trap air, keeping birds warm. Birds regularly use their bills to rearrange, or preen, their feathers. Why do they do this?

Obtain a flight or contour feather. You can find feathers in areas where waterfowl congregate. Use Figure 31 as a guide to feather anatomy. Separate one barb of a contour feather from another barb between your fingers (pull gently on the outer margin just below the top of the feather). Hold the feather up to a strong light and use your magnifying glass to examine the space between the individual barbs. Note that these spaces are filled with minute structures called barbules that crisscross at opposite angles.

Spread individual barbs on the feather vane. Now run the feather vane back through your fingers (from the bottom toward the top of the feather).

Use scissors to cut a piece of spread feather vane, and make a permanent mount preparation. Place the feather sample in the center of a clean microscope slide. Add two or three drops of corn syrup on top of the feather sample. Next, add

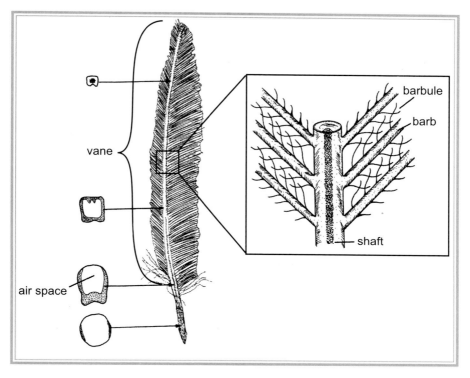

**Figure 31.** Contour feather anatomy.

a coverslip. Finally, use the eraser end of a pencil to push the coverslip down on the slide. Use a compound microscope at medium (100X) magnification to view barb and barbule structure. The barbules have tiny hooks that allow them to grab and hold barbs together.

## Science Fair Ideas

- Choose a large flight feather and hold the quill (shaft) toward you. Examine it with a magnifying glass. Notice a small hole that allowed the entrance of blood vessels to nourish the feather during life. Obtain a large sewing needle and gently push it up into the shaft. What do you observe? Is what you find a benefit to the bird? Now take a vegetable peeler and carefully shave the quill to obtain fine sections (shavings). Use fine tweezers to place a thin section in a drop of water on a microscope slide to make a section mount preparation (see Appendix A). Examine using a compound microscope and draw what you observe in your notebook. If possible, take a fingernail clipping and make a permanent mount preparation. Do both appear similar?

• Coloration results from chemical pigments and from the refraction of light from the structural irregularities of the feathers. Red, yellow, brown, and black are due to pigment, and blue and iridescent colors are caused by light refraction. White occurs when no pigment is present and the barbs equally reflect all wavelengths of light.

Use a magnifying glass to examine various colored feathers. Do your observations confirm the above statements?

Exploration 5.4

# How Old Do Fish Get?

**Materials**

* fish
* fish scales
* fine tweezers
* microscope slide
* eyedropper
* corn syrup
* coverslip
* pencil with eraser
* compound microscope, with light source

Few fish live longer than twelve years. Usually fish that grow longer than 30 cm (1 foot) have a lifespan of at least four or five years, although some fish, like the sturgeon, can live as long as fifty years!

Fish scales have an exposed portion that you can see and an embedded portion under the skin. There are four main types of fish scales. Most bony fish have ctenoid (rounded; smooth exposed area) or cycloid (oval-shaped; rough exposed area) scales. Others, like the sturgeon and gar have ganoid (diamond-shaped) scales. Sharks have placoid (pointed, tooth-shaped) scales. Some catfish and a few other fish species have no scales at all.

You can use Figure 32 as a guide, along with a compound microscope, to determine the age of a fish. If possible, visit the market and obtain some specimens—you can always catch a few fish, too! The ctenoid scales of perch are best to begin with.

Carefully remove scales from a body of a fish using fine tweezers. Allow the scales to dry. Use tweezers to place a dried scale in the center of a clean microscope slide. Use an eyedropper to obtain some corn syrup and carefully place a pea-sized drop directly on the dry specimen. Carefully lay the coverslip down on the drop. Gently spread the drop outward by applying gentle pressure to the center of the coverslip using the eraser end of a pencil.

Observe this permanent mount first at medium (100X) magnification to identify the scale type. Identify year growth

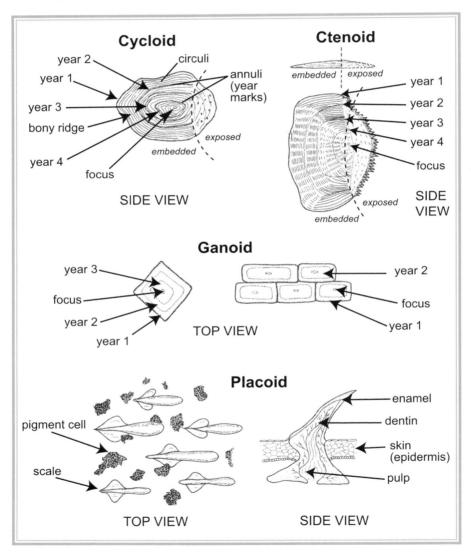

**Figure 32.** Fish scale types.

marks, or annuli. They will appear as lines around the portion of the scale that grew under the skin. When growth subsides in winter, a very small portion of the scale at the outer edge is absorbed by the fish. As growth begins again in the spring, it leaves a noticeable ring more obvious than the previous bony scale ridges, the ringlike markings, or circuli. One annulus (year mark) is formed each year.

Now examine the circuli. They reveal important information about growth periods and environmental and external factors that can affect growth. For example, if overcrowding, reduction of food, or unusually low temperature conditions exist, individual scale ridges will be smaller and closer together. Also look for a lack of scale ridges. These cutoffs indicate a cessation of growth.

You might want to examine several scales from the same fish, since fish often lose scales, and the replacements start out with no growth rings.

## Science Fair Idea

What do you and sharks have in common? Shark scales (placoid scales) are like your teeth—both have a cap of dentin that encloses a pulp cavity and is itself covered by hard enamel (see Figure 32). Fish markets usually carry shark steaks, which still has sharkskin attached. Run your fingers over the skin. Does it feel coarse, like sandpaper? Use a magnifying glass to examine sharkskin closely. You will see the spines of numerous placoid scales embedded in it. Use tweezers, while looking through your lens, to remove several scales. Allow them to dry. Make permanent mounts. Observe under a compound microscope at medium (100X) magnification.

# Exploration 5.5

# How Does a Spider's Web Trap Insects?

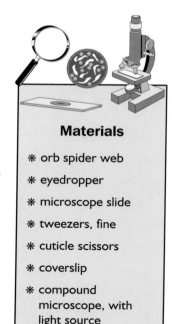

**Materials**

* orb spider web
* eyedropper
* microscope slide
* tweezers, fine
* cuticle scissors
* coverslip
* compound microscope, with light source

Orb weaver spiders construct the most beautiful and complicated webs. They weave circular webs in open areas, often between tree branches or flower stems. First, threads of dry silk are laid from the web's center, like the spokes of a wheel. Later, the orb weaver will lay down coiling lines of sticky silk that connects the spokes and serves as the insect trap. When this trapping silk is touched, it adheres to the object touching it. Use Figure 33 as a guide to spider webs.

Locate an orb weaver's web. Add a drop of water to a clean microscope slide. Use fine tweezers to hold a small section of coiling line. Use cuticle scissors to cut a section from the web. Make a wet mount by carefully lowering the piece of coiling line to the water drop. Add a coverslip.

Using the microscope, examine the wet mount under medium (100X) magnification. Since spider web material is transparent, increase the contrast by closing the disc or iris diaphragm. Compare your observations to Figure 33. Can you determine which parts of the coiling line are the sticky and which are elastic and stretch?

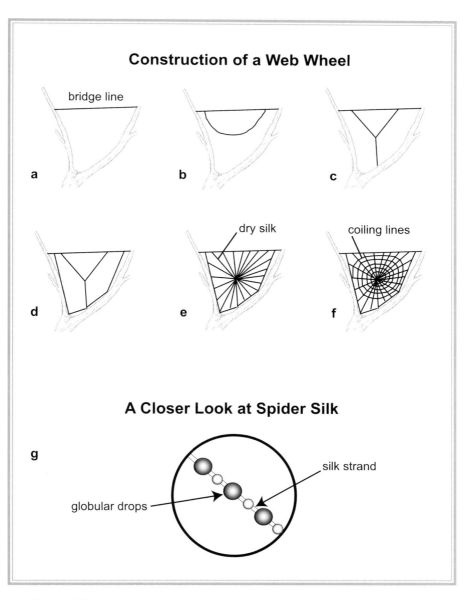

**Figure 33.** SPIDER WEBS AND SILK. a) The orb spider releases a sticky thread that is blown by the wind and carried to a spot where it sticks to form a "bridge line." b) A loose dry thread is then constructed. c) Next, Y-shaped radii are constructed. d–e) Additional dry threads are positioned to create a frame and other radii. f) Coiling lines of sticky silk are laid connecting the spokes to finish the orb web. g) Microscopic look at coiling line.

*Microscope Science Projects and Experiments*

## Science Fair Ideas

- Make a wet mount of a small portion of a spider's web. Are there optical differences between the "dry" and "sticky" silk types? Under the microscope, make comparisons using bright-field, dark-field, and polarized lighting illumination (see Appendix A).

- Wherever a spider goes, it spins a silk thread behind itself. This thread is called a dragline. Dragline silk is one of the toughest natural materials known to man.

    Collect dragline silk and make a wet mount of it. Compare dragline silk to the "dry" and "sticky" silk in an orb weaver's web—using bright-field, dark-field, and polarized light techniques described in Appendix A. Try comparing dragline and web silks from various spiders such as:

    –the grass spider (*Agelena naevia*), which weaves a funnel-shaped web in grass;

    –the triangle spider (*Hyptiotes cavatus*), an orb weaver that constructs triangular-shaped webs between twigs;

    –the common house spider (*Achaearanea tepidariorum*), which constructs a loosely woven tangled web of dry silk held in place by long threads attached to walls and other supports.

106

# Appendix A:

# Microtechniques

$M$*icrotechniques* are ways of preparing specimens for microscopic observation. These techniques will help you get the most out of your time with the microscope.

## Moving Solutions

*Useful for* introducing a stain or another solution to microlife-forms or cells under a coverslip in a wet mount.

### What You Do

Cut or tear a triangle-shaped piece(s) of paper towel. Use an eyedropper to place a drop(s) of stain or solution on one side of the coverslip, so that it just mixes with

| Moving Solutions Materials |
|---|
| * wet mount preparation |
| * paper towels |
| * eyedropper |
| * stain or other solution |

the existing fluid of the wet mount. Carefully insert one point of the paper towel piece underneath the opposite side of the coverslip. Watch as the liquid moves from one side of the coverslip to the other.

You may need to place additional drops of stain or use another paper towel piece to complete the introduction of stain or another solution under the coverslip. See Figure 34.

## Section Mount

*Useful for* mounting and staining tissue sections.

Safety: Use care when working with stains. Avoid skin and eye contact. Wear eye and hand protection.

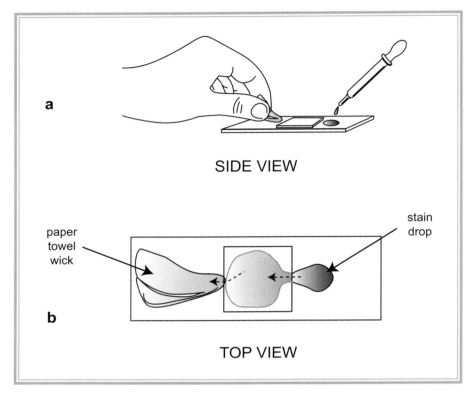

**Figure 34.** MOVING SOLUTIONS. a) Side view—add a drop of the solution you want to introduce. b) Top view—use a paper towel wick to replace one solution with another.

## What You Do

- Sectioning soft plant tissues: **Ask an adult** to show you how to use a vegetable peeler to obtain very *thin* slices or sections. With Figure 35 as a guide, use tweezers to pick up a thin plant tissue section and place it on a clean microscope slide. Add a contrast stain (optional) or a drop of water. Carefully add a coverslip. Use the low-power scanning (4X) objective to begin your search.

- Sectioning woody plant tissues: Practice using a hand pencil sharpener to create pencil wood shavings. Use tweezers to place a small wood shaving on a clean microscope slide. You may need to add additional drops to wet the wood shaving. Carefully add a coverslip. Use the low-power scanning (4X) objective to begin your search.

In sectioning actual plant branches, select and trim a branch that has a diameter similar to that of a pencil (8 mm, or 5/8 inch).

You can also ask an adult to use a carpenter's plane to make wood shavings for you to examine. Use a paper punch to stamp out small wood shaving circles to examine as a wet mount at low (40X) and medium (100X) magnification. Be sure to adjust the iris or disc diaphragm to allow as much light as possible through your wood section.

| Section Mount Materials |
| :--- |
| * an adult |
| * vegetable peeler, new |
| * soft plant tissues: celery, carrot, stems, roots |
| * tweezers |
| * glass microscope slide |
| * eyedropper |
| * methylene blue stain (optional) |
| * coverslip |
| * hand pencil sharpener, multi-size, new |
| * wood tissues: pencil, wooden dowels, small woody stems, wood blocks |
| * carpenter's plane |
| * paper punch |
| * disposable plastic gloves |
| * safety goggles |

## Staining

*Useful for* adding contrast to transparent organisms and tissues.

**Safety: Use care when working with biological stains. Avoid skin and eye contact. Wear eye and hand protection.**

Most living tissues and microorganisms are transparent, so adding contrast (a range of color) can help you see an object. Good contrast allows for the observation of fine detail at a particular magnification.

### What You Do

Obtain biological stains from your science teacher. Loeffler's methylene blue stain (0.1 percent) or iodine (one drop mixed with a drop of water on a slide) is excellent for adding contrast to most

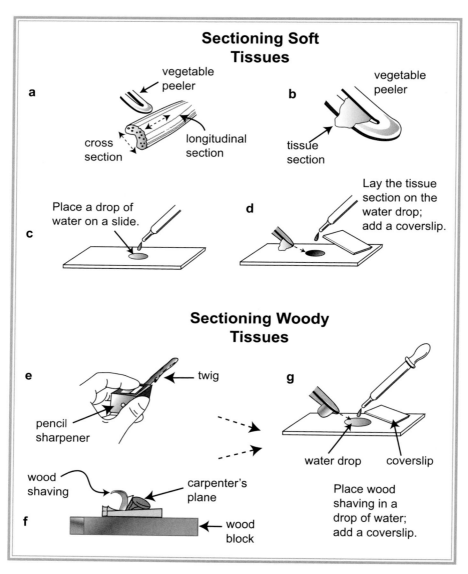

# Sectioning Soft Tissues

a — vegetable peeler — cross section — longitudinal section

b — vegetable peeler — tissue section

c — Place a drop of water on a slide.

d — Lay the tissue section on the water drop; add a coverslip.

# Sectioning Woody Tissues

e — twig — pencil sharpener

f — wood shaving — carpenter's plane — wood block

g — water drop — coverslip — Place wood shaving in a drop of water; add a coverslip.

**Figure 35.** MAKING SECTION MOUNTS. SECTIONING SOFT TISSUES: a) Use a new vegetable peeler to make longitudinal or cross sections of plant tissue. b) Try to obtain the thinnest section possible. c) Add a drop of water to a clean slide. d) You may need to add additional drops of water (or a stain) as well as a coverslip. SECTIONING WOODY TISSUES: e) Use a new pencil sharpener to make sections of a cylinder-shaped specimen such as a twig. f) Use a carpenter's plane to make thin sections of a flat piece of wood. g) Place a small piece of sectioned woody plant tissue in a drop of water on a clean microscope slide; add a coverslip.

transparent biological materials. Crystal violet stain (0.1 percent) is also excellent for staining bacteria.

In a pinch you can use food coloring. Mix one drop food coloring with a drop of water on a slide.

## Squash Smears

*Useful for* examining thick tissue specimens.

**Safety: Use care when working with biological stains. Avoid skin and eye contact. Wear eye and hand protection.**

### What You Do

Use tweezers to place the tissue on a clean microscope slide.

Use an eyedropper to add a drop of water over the tissue. Then add either crystal violet or methylene blue stain to the tissue. Place a coverslip on top of the tissue. Position the eraser end of a pencil on top of the tissue under the coverslip. Carefully apply a small amount of pressure, and at the same time give the pencil a slight twist, to squash and spread the tissues. Make sure that the tissues are separated; if not, repeat the squash procedure. This technique also works well with root hairs—see Exploration 4.1.

Examine the tissue at its edges under high (430X) magnification. Concentrate your attention on areas having thin tissue layers. They will have the fewest number of cells, so they will offer the best view.

| **Squash Smears Materials** |
| --- |
| * sample material |
| * tweezers |
| * glass microscope slide |
| * eyedropper |
| * crystal violet or methylene blue stain |
| * plastic coverslip |
| * pencil with eraser |
| * compound microscope, with light source |
| * disposable plastic gloves |
| * safety goggles |

# Hanging Drop Preparation

*Useful for* observing very small swimming microlife forms, including bacteria.

## What You Do

Use a toothpick to apply petroleum jelly along the outside of the circular depression slide. Apply a small drop of sample to the center of the coverslip using an eyedropper. Quickly invert the coverslip so that the drop hangs, then carefully lower the coverslip into contact with the petroleum jelly barrier. This creates a watertight seal and prevents the sample

| **Hanging Drop Materials** |
| --- |
| ✳ toothpick |
| ✳ petroleum jelly |
| ✳ depression slide |
| ✳ eyedropper |
| ✳ coverslip |

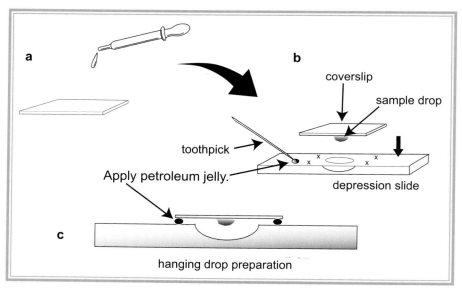

**Figure 36.** Making a hanging drop preparation. a) Add a single drop of material to a clean coverslip. b) Prepare a depression slide to receive the coverslip—apply small dabs of petroleum jelly where the coverslip will touch the slide. Quickly invert the coverslip so that the drop hangs. Carefully place the inverted coverslip over the well to rest on the applied dabs of petroleum jelly. c) A side view of the preparation shows a suspended hanging drop.

from evaporating. Microorganisms can be observed for days in a hanging drop (see Figure 36). Use this technique with dark-field illumination lighting.

## Slowing Down Fast-Moving Microlife

An excellent way to slow down fast-moving microlife-forms, such as the ciliate *Paramecium*, without using harmful chemicals is to use a toothpick to mix a drop of pond water or culture with a drop of 1 percent polyethylene oxide (1 gram slowly dissolved in 100mL very warm water; it forms a very thick solution). With a molecular weight of 4 million, it's like placing an individual in a room full of balloons—they are slowed down, but not drugged (see supplier 9 in Appendix B).

## Collecting Aquatic Organisms— Microbe Traps

*Useful for* observing biofilms.

Use various materials (glass slides, plastic coverslips, pieces of screen or aquarium netting, and sponges) to attract biofilms.

### What You Do

- Squeeze the contents from sponges, attached to stakes and left in various water environments (streams, ponds, and puddles) for several weeks, into a jar. Make wet mounts of the squeezings and examine under scanning (40X) and medium (100X) magnification.

- Make a small drift net sampler by stapling a 15-cm (6-in) square piece of window screen or aquarium netting to small 30-cm (12-in) sticks. Hold the sampler, with the netting touching bottom, downstream from an assistant who slowly stirs the bottom. This will release small organisms to be captured in the net (see Figure 37a).

- Use Figure 22 as a guide to making and setting out microbe traps. Make a group of microlife traps (small rectangular or circular plastic or acetate sheets held by clothespins) attached to a string. This string of traps can be set either vertically or horizontally by attaching it to a series of floats or floats and a weight.

Expose microlife traps for at least 2 weeks to collect bacteria and protists, and up to 4 weeks for micro invertebrates. Substrates like sponges should be left longer. Use toothpick scrapings (or squeezings) to make wet mounts for examination. Also examine surface films that accumulated on plastic coverslips by making wet mounts.

## Plankton Nets

*Useful for* collecting pond microlife.

### What you do

Using Figure 37b as a guide, cut off the end of a nylon stocking. Cut off the bottom of a 1-quart yogurt container. Then, slide the stocking over the yogurt container's opening and fasten it using staples or small rivets. Punch three equally spaced holes along the edge of the container, and attach the container to a towline. Use string or a rubber band to attach a clear plastic vial to the narrow end of the stocking.

> **Plankton Net Materials**
>
> * scissors
> * nylon stocking
> * 1-quart yogurt container
> * punch
> * towline
> * string or rubber band
> * staples or small rivets
> * clear, plastic vial

To collect specimens, either cast the tow net out and retrieve it, or drag it while walking along the shore or a dock or while riding in a slow-moving boat. As you collect samples, raise the net and allow the water to drain out. Then detach the vial with the concentrated sample. Study these concentrated samples.

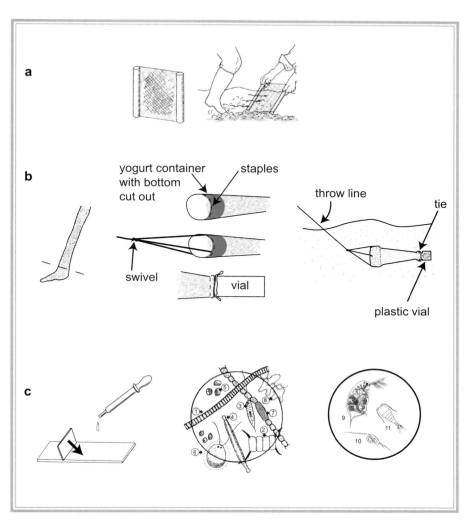

**Figure 37.** COLLECTING AQUATIC ORGANISMS. a) Make a kick net by stapling a piece of plastic window screening onto two dowels or thin pieces of wood about 61 cm (24 in) high. In a stream, place the kick net downstream of you. Gently stir up bottom debris—and hiding aquatic organisms—with your foot. Capture them in the screening for examination. b) Cut the foot off a nylon stocking. Attach the wider end of the stocking to the yogurt container using staples. Attach guidelines. Attach a small plastic vial to the smaller (cut) end of the stocking. Attach a throw line. c) After retrieving a water sample, make a wetmount. PLANKTON FORMS: 1) *Oscillatoria*, 2) *Scenedesmus*, 3) *Euglena*, 4) diatom, 5) *Chlorella*, 6) *Chlamydomonas*, 7) *Anabaena*, 8) net algae, 9) water flea (*Daphnia*), 10) rotifer, 11) copepod.

# Lighting Techniques

## Illumination and Magnifying Glasses or Single-lens Microscopes

*Useful for* magnifiers and other magnifying glasses.

The secret for better viewing is to restrict the lighting. The procedure, followed by the great microscopist Antoni van Leeuwenhoek, was to use light from a window (having a southern exposure) when viewing through his powerful magnifying glass. Such a small light source, he said, gave a clearer image.

Here are some viewing tips when using a magnifying glass (see Figure 38):

- Always try to reduce the cone of light that illuminates the object you are examining. You can do this by using a window, standing under a tree, or using a single light source (such as a desk lamp) when viewing. Position yourself so that you are looking at right angles to the light source. This viewing technique can be called side lighting.

- Sometimes direct lighting (a table lamp near the object to be viewed) is equally effective, especially when examining the printed word or a graphic image such as an engraving or photograph. This lighting provides a large amount of illumination.

- Another technique is to use interference lighting. Here the object to be viewed is placed directly between a light source and a lens. For example, hold an eggshell fragment up to a strong light to observe minute pores that allow for oxygen diffusion. Photographic negatives or transparencies require this type of lighting.

- Light-colored objects are best viewed over dark backgrounds (or in dark shadows). Similarly, dark-colored objects require light backgrounds.

- Very small objects are best viewed by holding them with tweezers or impaled on a pin.

- Do not remain still when peering through your lens. Move around! Try various lighting conditions and situations. Hold the object to be viewed in one hand and your magnifying glass in another. Constantly vary the illumination levels to obtain the best balance of light—or contrast—for viewing.

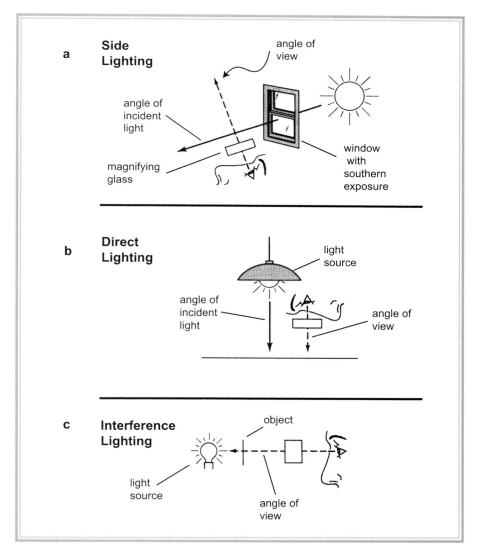

**Figure 38.** MAGNIFYING GLASS ILLUMINATION TECHNIQUES: a) Side lighting, b) Direct lighting, c) Interference lighting.

Always remember: Never look through any lens pointed directly at the sun. It can severely damage your eyes!

## Bright-field Illumination

*Useful for* any compound microscope with a mirror or built-in light source.

Bright-field microscopy involves using white light to view a magnified image—the usual way of viewing objects.

### Good Contrast Is Important

Contrast is the range of tones (e.g., grays or colors) in an image. Good contrast allows for the observation of fine detail at a particular magnification. Low- or high-contrast conditions in the specimen shift these range of colors.

Generally, if a single beam of white light is passed through a transparent specimen, little internal detail can be observed. A contrast stain must either be applied to the specimen, or a contrast illumination technique, such as dark-field or optical staining, must be used. (Note that these illumination techniques require a microscope having a substage condenser; see Figure 7).

To increase contrast, reduce the diaphragm opening (aperture). Reducing the opening darkens the specimen relative to its bright background. Unfortunately, the increased contrast is accompanied by a loss of resolution and color. Experiment to find the best compromise between resolution and contrast.

## Interference Lighting

*Useful for* any compound microscope.

Use an index card, placed over half a microscope illuminator, to create a partial "light stop" that interferes with the light path. This will create a high-contrast field of view. This illumination technique is very useful in observing transparent objects like cell structures carried by cytoplasmic streaming.

## Dark-field Illumination

*Useful for* any compound microscope having a substage condenser and filter holder.

Dark-field illumination microscopy is useful for obtaining the greatest level of image contrast. This is done by brightly illuminating the object while creating a black background (see Figure 39), which makes it easier to observe internal detail. Use of this

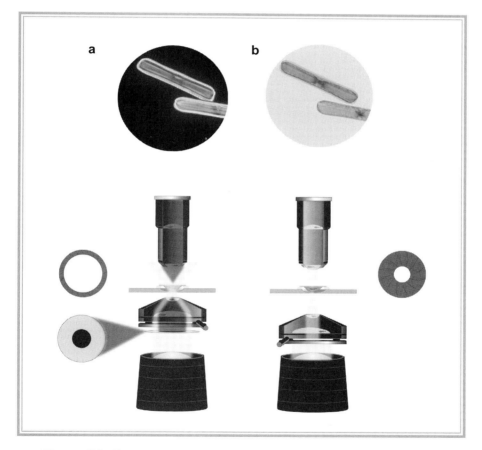

**Figure 39.** DARK-FIELD ILLUMINATION. a) Placing a dark-field light stop between the light source (or mirror) and the object to be viewed provides a brightly lit object viewed against a dark background (created by the light stop). You will need to have the iris diaphragm wide open. b) Without a light stop, the object and background are both brightly lit.

technique in combination with the hanging drop (an upside-down drop viewed from above) preparation provides for dramatic contrast views. A special dark-field light barrier or stop is used to create a black background. For example, living microlife-forms such as bacteria—which are not normally visible under bright-field microscopy—can be observed as light shimmers with dark-field illumination.

### Constructing dark-field light stops

Figure 40a contains a template for making light stops. Cut out a smaller central light barrier or stop out of black construction paper. Cut the larger support disk out of transparent acetate. Attach the light stop to the center of the acetate disk using clear tape. You may need to experiment with the size of the diameter of the light stop for best dark-field views. Place the dark-field light stop in the substage filter holder located below the condenser.

### Using dark-field illumination

Turn on the light source and place a wet mount or hanging drop preparation containing a transparent subject (e.g., pond life) on the stage. Open the iris diaphragm. As you look through the eyepiece, use the condenser control knob to move the condenser upward toward the stage. Focus the condenser until you observe the best darkened field of view.

## Optical Staining Illumination

*Useful for* any compound microscope having a substage condenser and filter holder.

Optical staining or Rheinberg illumination is useful in adding color to transparent specimens. This lighting technique is an extension of dark-field illumination. Here a transparent, colored, central light stop is positioned in the center of a larger colored or transparent light stop. The light stop is placed in the substage filter holder directly in the optical path of white light. The combination of these

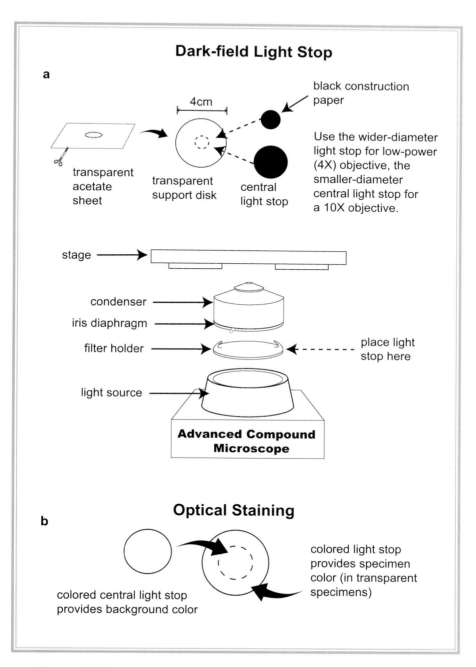

**Figure 40**. MAKING LIGHT STOPS. a) Making dark-field light stops. b) Making light stops for optical staining.

two light stops results in transparent specimens appearing in any color on a background field of any other color.

### Constructing light stops

Use Figure 40b as a guide in sizing and making light stops. Use colored acetate sheets available at art supply stores.

### Using optical staining illumination

Turn on the light source and place a wet mount or hanging drop preparation on the stage. Open the iris diaphragm. As you look through the eyepiece, use the condenser control knob to move the condenser upward toward the stage. Focus the condenser until you observe the best darkened field of view.

## Affordable Microscopes for Young Micronaturalists

Watch out for fantastic claims made by some manufacturers about the magnifying power of microscopes available in retail stores. Most times these viewing instruments have inferior lenses and poor illumination systems. A beginning microscopist will do fine with a microscope whose magnification range is between 5X and 200X. The microscopes below are available from the sources listed in Appendix B.

### Digital Computer Microscope

The QX3 computer microscope is capable of examining specimens or objects through the use of individual objective lenses that have magnification powers of approximately 10X, 60X, and 200X. The microscope is a single-lens type; there are no eyepiece lenses.

The software package that accompanies the QX3 microscope controls the microscope and excels in image capture and manipulation. Both consumer and school versions are available. Minimum system requirements: PC having USB connectivity; 200 MHz Pentium processor or faster with 32 Mb RAM and a 800 x 600 pixel display with 16-bit color depth (65,536 colors); Windows 98 or later. Mac with USB connectivity; OS 8.6 or higher (but not OS X).

## Barrel-Focus Compound Microscope

A barrel-focus compound microscope is a basic full-size compound microscope that allows the user to twist the body tube or barrel to focus. Instead of mirrors or electrical light sources, these microscopes use a unique light-gathering plastic, positioned under the stage, that concentrates light for reflected or transmitted light illumination—indoors or out. The microscopes use a single objective and eyepiece lens system, generally having a total magnification capability of 20X up to 200X.

## Single-Lens Handheld Microscope

Having a magnification ability of 16X, the Discovery Scope® is a commercial wide-field handheld magnifying glass. Its unique dark-tube optical pathway eliminates stray light, or flare, that can degrade an optical image. The secret to great micro or macro viewing is great lighting. Handheld portability allows the user to move the entire imaging system and the specimen into any light conditions they want. The user can easily get light to bounce off the front or side of the subject, or have light shine directly through the subject to observe internal details.

# Appendix B:

# *Science Supply Companies*

$M$ost of the materials required for projects in this book are available at local stores. However, if you wish to expand your home laboratory or obtain a hard-to-find life-form, the following firms offer science education materials. Generally chemicals must be purchased for you by your science teacher. Most companies can be contacted on the Web; some have web-based catalogs that will make direct ordering easy.

**1. Aldon Corporation**
*Chemicals and reagents for education*
1533 West Henrietta Road
Avon, NY 14414-9409
800-724-9877
<http://www.aldon-chem.com>

**2. Brock Optical, Inc.**
414 Lake Howell Road
Maitland, FL 32751
800-780-9111
<http://www.magiscope.com>

**3. BioMEDIA Associates**
*Unique audiovisual materials featuring freshwater and marine organisms*
P.O. Box 1234
Beaufort, SC 29901-1234
<http://www.ebiomedia.com>

**4. Carolina Biological Supply Company**
2700 York Road
Burlington, NC 27215
800-334-5551
<http://www.carolina.com>

### 5. Connecticut Valley Biological Supply Company

82 Valley Road
South Hampton, MA
01703
800-355-6813
<http://www.ctvalleybio.com>

### 6. Discovery Scope® Inc.

*Easy-to-use single-lens microscopes*
3202 Echo Mountain Drive
Kingwood, TX 77345
<http://www.Discoveryscope.com>

### 7. Edmund Scientific

60 Pearce Avenue
Tonawanda, NY 14150
800-728-6999
<http://www.scientificsonline.com>

### 8. Fisher Science Education

485 South Frontage Road
Burr Ridge, IL 60521
800-955-1177
<http://www.fisheredu.com>

### 9. Flinn Scientific

P.O. Box 219
Batavia, IL 60510-0219
800-452-1261
<http://www.flinnsci.com>

### 10. Frey Scientific

P.O. Box 8101
100 Paragon Parkway
Mansfield, OH 44903
800-225-3739
<http://www.freyscientific.com>

### 11. Neo/SCI Corporation

P.O. Box 22729
210 Commerce Drive
Rochester, NY 14692-2729
800-526-6689
<http://www.neosci.com>

### 12. Northwest Scientific Supply Ltd.

P.O. Box 6100 #310-3060
Cedar Hill Road
Victoria, BC V8T 3J5
Canada
250-592-2438
<http://www.nwscience.com>

### 13. Science Kit and Boreal Laboratories

777 East Park Drive
Tonawanda, NY 14150
800-828-7777
<http://www.sciencekit.com>

### 14. Urbana Laboratories

*Root nodule bacteria*
P.O. Box 1393
St. Joseph, MO 64502
816-223-3446
<http://www.urbana-labs.com/>

# Further Reading

Caduto, Michael J. *Pond and Brook: A Guide to Nature in Freshwater Environments.* Boston: University Press of New England, 1990.

Hershey, David R. *Plant Biology Science Projects.* New York: John Wiley & Sons, 1995.

Krieger, Melanie. *How to Excel in Science Competitions, Revised and Updated.* Berkeley Heights, N.J.: Enslow Publishers, Inc., 1999.

Levine, Shar, and Leslie Johnstone. *Fun With Your Microscope.* New York: Sterling Publications, 1999.

Rainis, Kenneth G. *Nature Projects For Young Scientists, Revised Edition.* Danbury, Conn.: Scholastic, 2002.

————. *Exploring with a Magnifying Glass.* Danbury, Conn.: Venture, 1995.

Rainis, Kenneth G., and Bruce J. Russell. *Guide to Microlife.* Danbury, Conn.: Franklin Watts, 1996.

## Internet Addresses

**Microbe Zoo.**
<http://www.commtechlab.msu.edu/sites/dlc-me/zoo/index.html>

**Optics For Kids.**
<http://www.Opticalres.com/kidoptx.htm#startkidoptx>

**Microscopy Society of America.**
<http://www.microscopy.com/>

# Index

ㄴ